THE BARONESS

UNMASKING HIMMLER'S

MOST SECRET AGENT

JOHN LUCAS

THE BARONESS

For Leonard

Contents

Foreword

The tale of Baroness Anja Bergroth Manfredi de Blasiis is not a typical spy story. It features little of the bravery or derring-do you might associate with the genre, and there are very few good guys. Rather, this previously untold story concerns a sickly, morally ambiguous oddball who may have had a significant influence over one of the main architects of the Holocaust in the final months of the war. It plunges us deep into the world of espionage in occupied Italy and beyond, as Nazi war criminals plotted a soft landing for themselves when the German war machine inevitably crashed. More often than not, these supporting characters did not get the justice they deserved.

Even though there are still so many unanswered questions about Anja's wartime activities, the tale is still worth telling. Anja faced a unique moral dilemma, with the desire to save her son by a Jewish ex-husband paving the way for her recruitment as a Nazi agent. Just how far she sympathized with her twisted paymasters will be for the reader to determine. At various points, Anja was suspected by the Italians of spying for Russia; by the Allies of spying for Germany; and by the Germans (some of them at least) of spying for the Italian resistance. Again, it will be up to the reader to decide where she might sit on the sliding scale between heroine, adventuress and criminal, and for whom she might really have been working.

Anja's case first came to light more than two decades ago, when MI5 declassified thousands of its World War Two records. But it has only ever been referred to fleetingly in barely a handful of history books, and then only in relation to the interrogation of her husband in Britain's Camp 020. His case in itself was significant, because it was crucial in determining whether or not intercepts decoded at Bletchley Park relating to Nazi plans for a post-occupation sabotage network in Italy were accurate. But Anja has always been brushed over as merely the wife of this obscure Italian baron, a woman who apparently met Himmler in a restaurant and fainted. As we shall see, there is much more to her story.

Until now, the most detailed account of the Anja Manfredi case appeared in the book titled *Camp 020*, with an introduction by Oliver Hoare, which was published by the National Archives back in 2000. Biographical information there was scant. Even taken together with the full MI5 files of her husband, Baron Manfredi, available at the National Archives in Kew, there was still not enough material to consider writing a book length story about this most mysterious of spies.

But the work of leading Finnish genealogist Peter Ragnvaldsson, who I contacted in early 2021, changed all that. His research allowed snippets of information to become fascinating narrative threads. For example, Anja's first husband was merely referred to in Manfredi's MI5 file as a Jewish man named "Goetz". Peter was able to attach a first name to this man and so open up the lamentable story of the suffering of the Götz family under Nazi rule. It is no exaggeration to say that this book would have been impossible to begin without his contribution. He also tracked down Anja's relatives in Finland and Sweden who, although they knew little about the woman herself, were able to supply a potted family history full of rich and intriguing detail. This was dramatically improved in early 2023 when American descendants of Anja's sister, Judith, got in touch having read the original version of this book. They had translated a family chronicle written in Swedish by Judith's son Kurt Stromfeldt in December 2000. It filled in many chronological gaps and provided huge amounts of colour.

In addition to thanking Peter, I'd also like to thank Kari-Matti Piilahti, of Finland's Family History Association, for putting me in touch with him in the first place.

Likewise, I must thank the relatives of Baron Manfredi who provided snippets of information which, although sparse, enabled certain points to be expanded.

Thanks also go to Christian Nunn at the Baden-Wuerttemberg State Archives in Karlsruhe, for his patience and help in obtaining documents that, in a story sometimes short on definitive endings, provided crucial insight into what happened to Anja after the war.

Family Drama

Fresh blood pools thick and dark on fine parquet floors. Anja Bergroth learnt this at a young age. She also learnt that when men fight, it isn't neat, tidy, or well-choreographed, like a boxing match or a duel from one of the novels she loved to read. It is nasty, chaotic, vicious, and — at least in the example that taught her these things — quite interminable.

Anja was only fourteen years old on the day her father unexpectedly fired a volley of gunshots at her sister's fiancé. And as both men desperately scrabbled around on the otherwise immaculately polished boards for control of the pistol, she learnt another thing — some people are utterly helpless in a crisis, while others are decisive.

Of the two antagonists, the most notable was Anja's father, Oskar Gideon Bergroth. It would not have been lost on her, even at such a young age, that this seemingly violent maniac was one of the most well-respected members of Finland's establishment, a senior prosecutor and high-ranking Freemason, and that such outrageous behaviour was well beneath him.

Oskar had come a long way from relatively humble beginnings. He was born on July 23, 1864, in the remote village of Kylmäkoski, in south west Finland, where his father Johan was the parish priest, as his father had been before him.[1] It was a joke passed down through the generations that when a local pastor died, the cry would go up amongst the peasants: "When will they choose a new Bergroth?" The surname itself meant something akin to mountain root, as at one point in ancient history a family farm had sat at the foot of a mountain. It was not a pretty name, and to compound matters Oskar was given a rather unflattering nickname – "Ugly Bergroth". Although by any measure, Oskar was not particularly unattractive, his daughter Judith would later write that he "was actually so ugly that people would view him with stunned surprise, almost with admiration….That family, anyway, was considered to be Finnish and there was evidence of this in Papa's round Mongol skull with slanty watery-blue pig eyes behind his rolls of fat".

Judith also gave some idea of the hardship Oskar would have endured as the son of a rural Finnish priest who believed very strongly in corporal punishment:

[Oskar was] just as ugly as his own father, with a strong and noticeable ugliness. A Finnish Lutheran with a sharp, penetrating gaze under white tufts of hair, a mouth so unexpectedly narrow and grim in that… fat face with the ample double chin, the white hair that fell over his temples in straight tufts. No, it was certainly no fun to be the object of his Lutheran anger. My father has told that, as a child, he had to stand during meals and kiss his father's hand and after Grace to thank him for the food. He also had to kiss him on hand after being spanked. The switch [wooden rod] hung behind the tile stove in his father's study and when punishment was to take place the delinquent had to push the chair up to the stove, climb up on it and take down the switch, unbutton his pants and assume the proper posture before the pastor, who whipped him in the name of the Lord.

Oskar chose not to follow the family calling and later obtained a master's degree in law from the University of Helsinki. He went on to practise in the city to some considerable success.

Oskar's social standing was enhanced by his marriage into one of Europe's most famous noble families. His wife, and Anja's mother, Sigrid Rosina Winter, was born on May 8, 1864, in Hartola, a municipality about a hundred miles north of the capital. She was the daughter of a protestant pastor, Adolf Magnus Winter, and Julia Malvina Bonsdorff, a scioness of the illustrious Bonsdorff family, best known for producing clerics and academics. Julia's father, Nils, had been a priest, and the pair met after Adolf became his assistant. One of Sigrid's eight siblings, Hugo Winter, was also ordained and he later officiated at Oskar and Sigrid's wedding. It was, without doubt, a large and most godly family. But the Winter children were not all saints, and in adult life politics drove a wedge between them.

Until the Finnish War of 1809, Finland had been part of Sweden for around seven hundred years. But after the conflict, Finland was subsumed into the Russian Empire and recast as a Grand Duchy with the Czar as Grand Duke. Resulting civil tensions spawned the Finnish nationalist movement. Finnish peasants typically spoke Finnish, while the language of the upper and middle classes, and thus the language of culture, education and civil administration, had always been Swedish.

This linguistic apartheid was encouraged by Russia to prevent the people uniting against its rule. It wasn't until the 1860s that Russia allowed Finnish to be incorporated into public life, and even then it took another three decades for it to become an official language. In the meantime, well-to-do Finnish nationalists from Swedish-speaking backgrounds who wanted to show they were on the side of the people began to speak Finnish.

One of Sigrid's eight siblings, Maila, was born in 1871, just as tensions over issues of liberalism, nationalism and language were heating up. Maila went on to become one of Finland's most famous writers, under the name Maila Talvio, and published works mostly about temperance, for which she was nominated three times for the Nobel Prize for Literature.

According to family legend, Maila was also "far right and a Finn zealot" who founded the first Finnish-language high school. The siblings all grew up together in a Swedish-speaking vicarage, but she opted to speak Finnish. On one occasion, gripped by revolutionary zeal, Maila flew into a rage after a meeting at their home where her father and other nobles spoke Swedish, even though the ordinary people present, including farmers and crofters, could not understand what was being said. It was arrogant and elitist, she believed, and a personal embarrassment. Maila later sealed her reputation as a Finnish-peasant national romantic, according to family lore, when she married the renowned Finnish linguist, Professor Jooseppi Julius Mikkola.

In contrast, brother Hugo was passionately pro-Swedish. In December 1894 Maila wrote him a letter which, while written in Swedish, had been addressed in Finnish. This provoked an explosive reaction from the priest. Brother and sister continued to converse only in their own chosen languages for the rest of their lives.

The row was typical of Hugo, whose stubborn and curmudgeonly nature was the stuff of legend. He was known for walking the streets with his eyes fixed on the ground, ignoring locals and their fruitless attempts to greet him. He could be equally aloof when it came to interactions in his own home, hating to socialise for its own sake. He only really had time for people who shared his faith, but even then, when a bishop proposed to visit it was arranged in advance that the meeting would last no longer than two hours. Much to the bishop's embarrassment, Hugo pedantically turfed him out after precisely a hundred and twenty minutes.

Perhaps surprisingly, given his miserly character, Hugo travelled widely, including to the United States, and gave lectures and wrote newspaper articles about what he had seen. He also wrote two books about his experiences. Hugo made at least one trip to Egypt with his uncle, the mathematician and scientist Ernst Jakob Waldemar Bonsdorff, and also visited Shanghai, Hawaii, Uruguay, Australia, Algeria, South Africa and the West Indies. According to family lore, Hugo once claimed to have had a ticket to board the Titanic but missed the journey because his train was delayed. He finally married at the age of sixty-three to his housekeeper, a woman ten years his junior. According to family legend, as they set off on their honeymoon the bride asked Hugo if he had the tickets. "I've bought mine," he replied, apparently not joking. They spent their entire — relatively short — married lives residing at opposite ends of the vicarage.

Another of Sigrid's siblings with literary ability was Ernst, who later styled himself Erkki West. Ernst grew up to be a sea captain and then wrote two books about his experiences. Meanwhile, sister Hedwig became a kindergarten teacher and later traveled to France, where family legend has it that she showed up to parties with a mysterious toyboy named La Trasse on her arm. Another sister, Lydia, became an artist who, somewhat controversially, married a Russian-born cello player, professor and legal consultant at the Ministry of Finance, named Nikolai Dobrohotov. When Oskar was posted to the government's offices in St Petersburg, Rosa took lessons to improve her already quite proficient piano playing, and enjoyed collaborating with Dobrohotov, who filled the family home with chamber music. The Bergroth family moved back to Helsinki in about 1907, after Rosa's language teacher was found to be a revolutionary and Oskar deftly talked the authorities out of sending them all to Siberia.

Another of the Winter sisters became famous for very different reasons. Anna Helena Winter married a man named Carl Erik von Gerdten in 1885, but he later died unexpectedly. Anna's mother-in-law alleged that the wife had poisoned her son with arsenic. There was a trial and the body was sensationally exhumed, but Anna was acquitted in court.

***

Oskar and Sigrid welcomed their first child, Judith Valborg Bergroth, into the world on January 28, 1896. Another daughter, Ann-Mari, was born in 1898 but died just three months later. British intelligence officers later referred to the couple's second surviving daughter, Anja Elisabeth, born June 17, 1901, as Anna Maria, suggesting that she might have co-opted her deceased sister's name at some point. In any case, she was nicknamed Aja by her family.

Both Judith and Anja were a little plump and round-faced, like their father, but also inherited their mother's striking looks. A photo from the official Bonsdorff family history shows them as teenagers, both gazing into the camera with large dark eyes, their cheeks inches apart, each girl's dark mop of hair bleeding into the other. They were clearly close, and apart from their similar looks both girls would have enjoyed all the privileges to be expected in the home of one of Helsinki's leading families.[2]

Yet despite no doubt having access to the best tutors in Helsinki, Judith failed to live up to her father's academic expectations. In 1914 he complained to the New Swedish Co-educational School that his daughter had not been allowed to enroll for her pre-university year, despite being admitted the previous term. The sticking point seemed to be that she had done poorly in her maths exams. The dispute itself made the newspaper, and although the eventual outcome was not published, it's unlikely that Oskar would have been refused.

No doubt a key reason behind Judith's academic malaise had been the death from cancer of her mother the previous September. Both girls were devastated to lose their mother at such a young age. And as for Oskar, even with a bevy of servants and tutors to help around the house, the prospect of raising two daughters by himself must have been daunting. No doubt he was keener than ever to see his girls succeed. Crucially, Oskar might have been desperate to see Judith go off to university because in the meantime she had fallen in love with an older man.

Aged eighteen, Judith had begun courting a promising medical student named Gunnar Aspelin. It would have been all well and good, if not for the fact that he was fourteen years her senior and a divorcee, with a daughter about Judith's age. Oskar opposed their subsequent engagement, despite Gunnar's good prospects, and forbade the pair to meet, although he also sent mixed signals. On one occasion, when Oskar saw him in the street, he asked a slightly baffled Gunnar why he had stopped calling on him socially. Glad to be back in the fold, the student duly took him up on his offer.

Unfortunately, Oskar was not home when the younger man showed up a few days later. By this point, Oskar had risen to become Helsinki's district chief prosecutor, a very senior position that commanded respect. There would have been no reason for Gunnar to fear a violent reaction. However, when Oskar arrived home he heard Gunnar in Judith's room and the red mist began to descend. Judith appeared to be absorbed in a book when Oskar poked his head around the door, and Gunnar was sat nonchalantly in a chair, reading a newspaper. But suspicious and silently fuming, Oskar withdrew into his own room, and after fifteen minutes shouted, "What are you doing here?"[3]

Bemused by this outburst, Gunnar went into Oskar's study, but without warning Oskar pulled out a revolver and fired two shots. The first missed, but the second bullet struck Gunnar's arm, passing straight through and lodging in the muscle around his hip. Oskar would surely have fired a third and fatal round if Gunnar had not lunged forwards and dragged him to the floor, where they spent ten minutes or so wrestling. In the scramble, another shot was indeed let loose, grazing Gunnar's neck. Judith looked on helplessly, screaming at the pair to stop as they sloshed around in Gunnar's blood. It was the fourteen-year-old Anja who acted decisively. Realising that someone would soon end up dead, she fled the house and ran for help. The police arrived within minutes and managed to wrest the revolver from Oskar's grip. As Anja grew older, her ability to remain cool under pressure would see her through many tough times.

Astonishingly, Oskar faced no punishment for what many felt was a clear attempt to murder his daughter's lover — the charge of pre-meditation seemingly obvious on account of the fifteen minutes Oskar had spent ruminating before firing the gun. While all the parties were questioned by police, no trial took place and Oskar remained a free man. Still, the incident must have been extremely shocking to both Judith and Anja, and appears to have permanently undermined Oskar's relationship with them both.

Despite her father's extreme aversion to the match, Judith married Gunnar in April 1916. The wedding reception, if attended by Oskar, would have been interesting to say the least. But the union didn't last, even though Judith and Gunnar's only child, a daughter named Ruusu, was born seven months later. The couple divorced after a decade together and Judith moved to Blankensee, in Germany, where she married her second husband six months after that. Kurt Ludvig Antonio Meyer-Stromfeldt, a successful lawyer, was also on his second marriage. The couple had two children, Anja (nicknamed Itschi) Meyer-Stromfeldt, born in 1928, and Curt Antonio Meyer-Stromfeldt, born in 1931.

Meanwhile, Anja became and accomplished piano player and was educated at home until the age of sixteen, before going on to study art history, literature and philosophy at Helsinki University. According to British intelligence files, she also "studied languages with considerable success".[4] At some point in the early 1920s Anja followed in her sister's footsteps and decamped to Germany, after going abroad for what was only supposed to be a holiday.

As Judith's son Kurt later wrote: "The Bergroth girls grew up into a pair of beautiful and accomplished young ladies. Both had a taste for adventure. This resulted in a social life that was altogether too free for the times, with boyfriends, restaurants etc., and, in connection with [Judith's] divorce from Gunnar Aspelin, scandal with echoes in the press….Helsinki became too small for the girls and they looked for work in Germany - namely, in Hamburg."

In the intervening period, Finland experienced the national trauma of the civil war of 1918, which saw White Finland nationalists, aligned with the Germans, take on Red Finland, backed by Soviet Russia, all against the backdrop of World War One and Finland's declaration of independence in 1917. It was a bewildering and highly charged time, when Helsinki was controlled by the Reds until the Germans and the Whites pushed through in late April 1918, with the subsequent battle claiming some five hundred lives. We know little of the role the Bergroth family played in the conflict, but given that Oskar continued to figure in Helsinki's high society after the war, we can safely assume he was not a

Bolshevik. In addition, Judith worked at Germany's military headquarters until November 1918, which suggests the family all had similar leanings.

The Battle of Helsinki left the city's streets littered with corpses, including in the suburban areas, while the conflict overall claimed the lives of some 36,000 Finns — roughly 1.2 percent of the population. Many of them died in prison camps, or in retaliatory attacks as the losers fled to Russia. The period would have been a terrifying time for Anja and probably served to galvanise her political views — every indication suggests that she grew up with no love lost for Communism and would most likely have been very pro-German, after all, it was the Germans who helped to liberate Finland. We don't know exactly how the political situation affected her wider family in material terms, although a British intelligence report on Anja would later state: "The family was at one time in a very good financial position but lost a considerable amount of their fortune through the Russo-Finnish Revolution of 1918."

As for Oskar, he had remarried a year after shooting Gunnar Aspelin, to Esther Maria Erich, who ironically was twelve years his junior. However, she died in 1921 and Oskar married for a third time two years later, to Anna Elisabeth Ytterberg. This time, the marriage came to an end when Oskar returned home from work one day to find the apartment stripped of furniture and a note from his wife informing him that she'd left for Sweden, where she lived until the 1960s. Oskar died in March 1934, at the age of sixty-nine. Despite his violent outburst several years earlier, he was still celebrated at his funeral as one of the nation's leading lawyers and described in subsequent newspaper reports as a "masonic Lord", which perhaps explains how he dodged the attempted murder charge. The occasion was attended by dozens of dignitaries, including the Finnish diplomat Onni Talas, who Anja would later describe as her uncle when they both lived in wartime Rome. Prominent members of the Bonsdorff and Lindroff families also turned up.

But among the long roll call of mourners there was no mention of either Judith or Anja attending the funeral. We can probably surmise why Judith might have avoided the occasion — it seems she had still not forgiven her father for shooting her ex-husband. But Anja also had a good reason to be bitter. Shortly after her trip to Germany, Anja informed Oskar that she planned to marry a Jewish businessman from Hamburg. Oskar furiously opposed the match on openly antisemitic grounds. But once again, a Bergroth girl was not going to be told what to do by her embittered old father.

Anja was going to marry whoever the hell she wanted.

---

[1] From Bergroth/Bonsdorff/Winter family history compiled by Peter Ragnvaldsson. All subsequent information in this chapter comes from the same source, unless stated otherwise.

[2] Bonsdorff, Axel, p.59.

[3] Blodsramat I Helsingfors. Åbo Underrättelser, September 29, 1915.

[4] Manfredi files, UK National Archives.

Mr and Mrs Götz

THE dark shadow of National Socialism failed to envelope Germany in November 1923, when Adolf Hitler's chaotic Beer Hall Putsch collapsed in a hail of bullets. Hitler was soon locked up and the Nazi threat looked to have been permanently neutered. Many Germans felt they had to more to fear from the Communists, who staged several uprisings that year, including in Hamburg, where nearly a hundred people died in rioting. But for Hans Götz, life had never been better. Business was good, despite the economic situation, and back in March he had married his wife, Anja Bergroth. Now they were planning to raise a family. Hans had no reason to believe that soon the Nazis would return to tear his world apart.

Hans Leopold Götz was born in Hamburg on October 8, 1896, to Oscar Benjamin Götz, the founder of a prestigious shipping company, and Agnes Götz, née Falk. Two years previously, Agnes had given birth to the couple's first boy, Werner, and in December 1905 she had another son, Reinold. Clearly the Götz clan was close, because in the same year that Hans was born, one of Agnes's sisters, Dorothea, married one of Oscar's brothers, Robert, a banker, later producing a daughter, Elsbet, and a son, Oswald. All the children were sent to the city's oldest Gymnasium, or Grammar School, the Johanneum. Although of Jewish ancestry, the entire Götz clan had converted to Christianity. The children, including Hans, were baptized Protestant.

The two Götz families lived in separate houses, although each property was only a stone's throw away. Oscar, Agnes, Werner, Hans and Reinold resided in a glorious riverside home at Leinpfad 22a. Robert, Dorothea, Elsbet and Oswald lived at Agnesstrasse 55. The two properties practically backed onto each other and family members were able to play and visit through a gate in the fence. The kids enjoyed a very happy childhood and Elsbet in particular grew up playing with her male cousins "almost like a boy" according to her niece, Renate Osthoff, who later contributed a potted history to a project remembering Hamburg's Holocaust victims.[5]

Renate was extremely fond of Elsbet, who she spoke of adoringly and gave the nickname "Fat," meant affectionately and in reference to her rounded figure. About one visit to Hamburg, Renate recalled, "After lunch everyone rested. We were allowed to take turns lying on her couch with Elsbet. She wore pearls in her earlobes and smelled wonderfully of perfume. We weren't allowed to say a word and we didn't....On her bookshelf there were books that we were 'not yet' allowed to read. I remember Lysistrata by Aristophanes, which I read secretly." There were unhappy moments. On one occasion, Judith Bergroth's first daughter Ruusu was trying to retrieve a ball from a glass conservatory roof when she fell through and broke her leg badly, an experience that apparently contributed to a troubled adult life.

Tragedy also struck the Götz family toward the end of World War One. Hans' older brother, Werner, was killed in battle, while Oscar died at home in 1918, aged fifty-three. Hans also fought in the war. Having graduated from school in 1914, he signed up the following year, before being discharged in 1918, apparently unscathed. British intelligence files suggest he was a lieutenant and served in Italy, and while we know little about his experiences during the war, the country must have left a deep impression on the young man, because he would later give his only son a distinctly Italian-sounding name.

After surviving the conflict that had claimed the lives of nearly 1.8 million Germans, Hans enrolled at the Technical University in Munich. It's not clear what he studied, but he may well have brushed past a fellow student who was studying agriculture there at the time — future SS chief Heinrich Himmler. It was a period when antisemitism was on the rise, with demagogues like Himmler still forming their views and in some cases inflicting their prejudices on fellow students. For whatever reason, Hans quit after just three months to return to Hamburg, where he studied arts and crafts before starting a book trade traineeship. It was the best decision he ever made.

Hans founded his own business, the eponymously-named antiquarian bookstore, the Bücherstube Hans Götz, in October 1920, initially based at Esplanade 451, close to both the harbour and the splendor of Dammtor Park. The bookstore catered for a wide variety of tastes, from new titles for the general retail customer, to a specialist ordering service for rare or out-of-print works, as well as graphic art. He also offered advice on compiling libraries, building collections and choosing gifts. Hans attracted customers by arranging author readings and, from 1922, he sent out hundreds of catalogues to collectors across Europe.[6]

It is easy to imagine Anja gravitating towards Hamburg in the 1920s, the city then known as Germany's gateway to the post-war world and an intellectual and cultural hub. There she would have found Hans' bookstore at the centre of Hamburg's literary life. At some point before the outbreak of World War Two, Anja found work as a journalist, but exactly when, where and for who, was never made clear in her files. In any case, she had an interest in literature and it's possible that Anja was a regular browser. Perhaps she attended an event either in a professional capacity, or simply for leisure, or maybe to scour the shelves for works by her own relatives, Erkki West, Hugo Winter, and Maila Talvio. We can only guess as to how the couple first met. Did Hans watch from afar before finally plucking up the courage to speak to Anja? Or was it the other way around? Perhaps she interviewed Hans for an assignment. What we know for sure is that at some point Anja and Hans began courting, because on March 28, 1923, they got married.

Anja's MI5 report tells the story very simply, merely stating that she met a man named "Goetz," a German Jew of "considerable means," while on a "holiday tour".[7] Her father, the spies added, was a "nobleman of an ancient family" and was strongly opposed to her marrying a Jew. Whatever the facts of their courtship, Anja duly became a German citizen and took with her a dowry of ten million Finnish marks.

On the face of it, the dowry was a sizable sum, but in 1923 the Weimar Republic was gripped by hyperinflation. Already by the time Hans and Anja married, the price of a loaf of bread had reached about 460 marks. By November, when the crisis was brought to an end, it had soared to 201,000,000,000 marks. However, the couple managed to weather this financial storm and it apparently did not affect Hans' thriving business, nor their plans to add a new member to their household.

The following year, on June 2, 1924, Hans and Anja were joined by a son, who they named Aldo Bodoni Götz. It is tempting to believe that Hans named him after a former comrade in Italy. At that time, neither Anja nor Hans had any other obvious connections to the country.

The stage appeared set for a long, happy family life. A contemporary photograph shows Anja and Hans standing together side-by-side, probably on a Hamburg street. She is wearing a wide-brimmed hat — casting her eyes in a thick black shadow — a fur coat, and a white scarf. Hans is wearing a smart homburg hat with a light band and round-framed spectacles. Another photo from the same Bonsdorff family album shows Anja alongside Aldo, much later, when the boy was probably a teenager in Italy. She appears slim and is dressed in a fur coat and stylish hat, slanted over her right eye. There is an assured half-smile on her face, while Aldo, in a cap and fez-style hat, looks pensive.[8] Of course by then, the Götz family had been well and truly shattered.

But before everything fell apart, the family business went from strength to strength. Hans added auctions to his bookstore's range of services in 1924, building a regular network of some 3,000 collectors who received his catalogues in the mail.[9] The same year, the bookstore moved to a larger venue to accommodate the events, which included presentations of graphic works by the Flemish pacifist Frans Masereel and the Austrian expressionist Alfred Kubin, whose art was later declared *entartete Kunst* or "degenerate art" by the Nazis. In total, the bookstore produced at least seventy catalogues up until 1934. Much of the store's success came from the national attention it received for the two-part auction of the library of the Danish Counts of Heiligenstedten, carried out on behalf of the provincial government of Schleswig-Holstein in 1927. There was also the auction of the library of the Counts of Blome in 1929, which earned Hans some RM70,000 in commission, and the auction of the Von Chorinski library, from the property of Count Franz von Sprinzenstein. Featuring rarities from the fields of medicine, alchemy and the occult, it brought collectors from far and wide and garnered Hans an international reputation, plus a commission of RM 1,000,000.

But by then the world was in a global depression. About 1.5 million Germans were out of work by the end of 1929, and the figure more than doubled within a year. By early 1933, unemployment in Germany had reached six million, equivalent to more than one-third of its working population. Bankruptcies and foreclosures spread like wildfire. Even more pressing, from Hans' point of view, were the maintenance payments he was now being forced to make to Anja.

We don't know why the marriage broke down, leading to a divorce in 1928, but according to later British intelligence reports, Hans was an "abnormal and feckless husband" who brought "horrors and ill-health" upon his wife. It's not entirely clear what any of this meant, and it had come solely from a second-hand source, namely Anja's second husband, who was told this tale by her. But it seems possible that Hans had an affair. Anja's family certainly thought she'd been playing away from home. Judith's son Kurt later wrote that Anja had "romances on the side". He wrote that Aldo spent much time living with his mother just outside Hamburg, and added: "He was very difficult child, who obviously had suffered some damage from his parent's broken marriage. There were many stories about his behavior."

On March 7, 1931, Hans became a father for the second time, to a girl named Maria, although if the German records for the birth still exist, they cannot be found. When Maria's name later appeared on the 1940 census in Denmark, the entry said Hans was a widower, even though, once again, there is no record of a marriage. According to the history written by Judith's son, the mother's name was Käthe.

It is conceivable that a journalistic lifestyle also helped to erode Anja's relationship with Hans. She might have spent many afternoons and evenings away from home, socializing and developing her contacts. Judging by a later list of associates compiled by British intelligence, Anja cultivated friendships with many people in the worlds of showbusiness and diplomacy. It's not clear exactly when or where she was employed. But if she did find work in Hamburg then the well-established *Hamburgischer Correspondent* is a possible contender. It was widely respected, although slanted towards the government, and in April 1934, with the Nazis firmly in power, it was forced to merge with the *Hamburger Nachrichten*, becoming the first paper to close under the regime. Then again, the city had more newspapers than anywhere else in Germany, including the *Hamburger Abendblatt*, the *Hamburger Morgenpost*, and the *Bild-Zeitung*. There were also weekly and monthly magazines issued by the various publishing firms located in the city.

If Anja wasn't working as a journalist before the split with Hans, then she was soon afterwards, according to British intelligence, who said she obtained work as a journalist and translator, which she found to be a "lucrative occupation" that helped her to support Aldo. MI5 apparently knew nothing of the maintenance payments, Hans' mounting debts, or his subsequent bankruptcy in August 1931.[10]

Going bankrupt meant that Hans was no longer able to trade under his own name, thereby forcing him to forego his stellar reputation forged over the previous decade. Hans had to subsist on a commission-only business and, from 1932-33, he organized auctions of aristocratic libraries for profit sharing with the antiques dealer Harry Hirsch, who lacked the knowledge to create his own catalogs. By mid-1933, nine such auctions had been held, followed in May 1934 by three further catalogs and a sales list for a private collection of children's books.

The Nazis triumphed in the Reichstag elections of July 1932, becoming the largest party with 230 seats. A passenger manifest from the SS Dewsbury shows Hans leaving Hamburg alone for London in

October that year, possibly only for work purposes, although perhaps he was ahead of the curve and looking for a new place to locate his business. In any case, Hans soon returned to Hamburg, where in 1934 he was forced to sign up with the *Reichsschrifttumskammer*, the books section of the Nazi's Reich Chamber of Culture, a twisted organisation tasked with 'Aryanising' German culture and excluding Jews from society. Its primary function was to check the suitability of members, by examining whether they had criminal records, were homosexual, or had Jewish ancestry. From 1934, Jewish members were expelled and their businesses appropriated.

Although baptized Evangelical Lutheran, Hans was deemed to be non-Aryan and so was ejected from the *Reichsschrifttumskammer*, meaning that he could no longer operate as a bookseller, dealer, or auctioneer. In other words, he was finished. With Maria in tow, Hans fled to Copenhagen, where he had plenty of contacts in the trade. However, he was forced to liquidate most of his stock and almost all of the proceeds were spent on shipping costs for the rest, so when he arrived in the Danish capital in 1935, Hans barely had a pfennig to his name. He couldn't obtain a work permit, so he had to wait it out in Malmo, Sweden, for three months, earning money through commission work for the Danish antiquarian bookseller Lynge and Son. Hans eventually secured a residence and work permit that enabled him to move to Copenhagen permanently.

But the Nazi horror quickly spread across Europe and Germany invaded Denmark in April 1940. Hans and Maria appeared on the census taken in November that year. At the time, they were living with a family named Ibsen in Brannersvej, Gentofte. For a while, nothing really changed and Hans was able to continue his work. But in October 1943, after more than three years of occupation, Himmler ordered the Jewish population to be deported. What happened next is one of the greatest acts of defiance of World War Two. The German attaché in Copenhagen, Georg Ferdinand Duckwitz, tried to halt the deportations and, after appealing to his superiors in Berlin, took the risky decision to tip off Danish and Jewish politicians, who in turn warned Jewish community leaders and organised the largest single rescue of Jews seen during the conflict. Around 7,200 Jews and another 700 relatives were helped to escape via fishing boats across the Oresund to Sweden. Hans Götz and Maria were among them.

Hans' surviving brother, Reinold, had also become a successful businessman. After taking up a commercial apprenticeship he went into the stamp dealing trade, forming the Marcophilhaus Reinold Götz company. But like Hans, he was ruined by the *Reichsschrifttumskammer*. In December 1938 he was living in Amsterdam, where he managed to get passage to the island of Trinidad, then still a part of the British Empire. Forced to sell his company, the meagre proceeds were entirely eaten up by the cost of the ticket. But he did live out the war in relative safety and in an agreeable Caribbean climate. Hans and Reinolds' cousin Oswald also fled Germany in December 1938, and survived the war. Yet the females of the family, Hans' mother Agnes, aunt Dorothea and cousin Elsbet, did not fare so well.

The Götz women left behind in Hamburg struggled against the rising tide of persecution. Initially, they survived on the family's existing wealth and were even able to take short holidays away from the city. But their so-called friends no longer wanted to know them and a private kindergarten Elsbet had opened in the Agnesstrasse house in the 1920s had to be closed. The family's 'Aryan' domestic servants were forced to quit by law, not being allowed to work in Jewish households, although one loyal maid, Hedwig, ignored the racial diktat.[11]

And then, on November 9, 1938, came Kristallnacht, the Night of Broken Glass, in which the Nazi paramilitary wing, the Sturmabteilung (SA), the Hitler Youth, and thousands of civilians attacked Jewish-owned businesses, homes, hospitals, schools and synagogues across the country. It was a national disgrace that left hundreds of Jews dead. In Hamburg, at least nine synagogues were attacked, including the city's largest on Bornplatz, and at least 900 Jews were arrested and imprisoned, most of them in the Gestapo-run Fuhlsbüttel concentration camp, others in Sachsenhausen.

In one case, a music teacher named Martin Cobliner died after falling from a window when police turned up to arrest him. By their account, he committed suicide rather than be captured. Hamburg resident Johanna Gerechter Neumann later recalled the violence and chaos of Kristallnacht in Hamburg. "What I saw were hordes of people standing in front of a beautiful synagogue and throwing stones through these magnificent colored windows. Jewish stores in the center of Hamburg had been demolished, windows had been broken, the merchandise had been thrown into the streets. It was a total chaos, a total destruction," she said.[12]

If Hans Götz had not already suffered the heartache of losing his business to Nazi appropriation, this was the fate that almost certainly would have befallen his bookstore, and the antiquities therein. The remaining Götz women and their property in Hamburg apparently remained unscathed by the shameful events of that night. Yet the nationwide mob rampage was merely a prelude to the horror that was to come.

Back in July of that year, all Jews had been forced to declare their assets exceeding RM5,000. Now, following the pogrom, the victims were made to pay for the damage caused, through a special tax, a measure announced just over a week later on November 21. They were given less than a year in which to pay a twenty percent levy on their property in four installments. The Nazis reserved the right to collect further payments if the total of one billion Reichsmarks was not reached by the following August. Predictably, the regime did indeed demand more money in November 1939.

The only way for most people to raise the cash, without losing their homes, was to sell off items such as jewellery and silverware, which Agnes, Dorothea and Elsbet did. Hans' cousin had kept up her correspondence with her niece, Renate, who later wrote of Elsbet's lament that it was now forbidden to go to the theatre or concerts. Elsbet amused herself by whistling the St Matthew Passion on Good Friday, telling Renate wryly, "If you know it so well, that may be enough."[13] Elsbet was keeping her spirits up, but things would only get worse.

Hans' mother Agnes tried in vain to transfer the family's remaining bank shares and the house to relatives in Frankfurt. But the Nazis had an answer for that as well. They demanded a fee of RM120,000, to be paid up front, before they would even consider approval. It was impossible to meet the demand and the house had to be relinquished. Agnes was forced to move in with Dorothea and Elsbet. More persecution followed. After 1940, the family was no longer allowed to have a telephone connection, although bookseller Greta Stolterfoht allowed the family to make calls from the back of her store. As a young and healthy woman, Elsbet Götz was ordered to work in forced labour factories, first making canned vegetables and then paper twine. Despite the slide into ever deeper misery, she was still looking for love. Elsbet picked up an enthusiastic admirer amongst the other slave labourers, writing to her niece: "Yes, the aunt has her charms! But now I have forbidden any further harassment."

Elsbet spotted an opportunity to escape the horror of Nazi Germany during a family trip to the Tyrol, near the Swiss border, in 1941. With the help of an Austrian friend, Elsbet crossed into the neutral territory but quickly returned, not wanting to leave her mother to face her fate alone. When the family returned to Hamburg, they were ordered to begin wearing the yellow Stars of David that the Nazis had so far only foisted upon the Jewish citizens of the occupied territories.

By the Autumn of 1941 there were still around 338,000 Jews who had either been unwilling or unable to flee the country. Hitler had so far resisted the urge to deport them to occupied territories because he feared it could spark a wave of popular anger against the regime, something he was not prepared to risk as the Nazi war machine continued to open up new fronts abroad. But it was something he planned to do as soon as the war was over. Other leading figures saw things differently. SS boss Himmler, sadistic security chief Reinhard Heydrich, and arch Jew-hater Adolf Eichmann all argued that it was better to be rid of the Jews sooner rather than later. Hitler was swayed and issued an order to begin deportations to the east that September.

Both Elsbet and her mother were due to be deported to Riga, Latvia, on December 6, 1941, but they were allowed to remain after Elsbet had an operation to remove her appendix on December 1. She successfully argued that she needed time to recuperate. Their names were crossed out by hand on the deportation list. But the reprieve was short lived. On July 19, 1942, Elsbet, Agnes and Dorothea boarded a train to Theresienstadt, a ghetto in Czechoslovakia. Like most of the deportees, they had been made to believe that the money from the forced sale of the house in Agnesstrasse would be used to buy them a place to live — and the right to eat — in the new land. But instead they were shunted into mass accommodation and left to fend for themselves.

Theresienstadt was established in November 1942 as a transit camp for Jews being shipped east, but at any one time until its liberation by the Red Army in May 1945 it held around 35,000 people. In total, around 33,000 people died there, and 88,000 were deported to concentration camps.[14]

Heydrich had chosen the former garrison town to be transformed into a settlement for German, Austrian and Czech Jews over the age of sixty-five, World War One veterans, and well-connected or famous cultural or political individuals — those with "special merit". The ghetto's library contained some 60,000 volumes and prisoners were drawn mainly from the classes of artists, poets, philosophers, writers, musicians, professors and scientists, many of them too elderly or too sick to be able to work. As a result of the type of inmate at Theresienstadt, a wealth of material, including paintings, poems, drawings, essays, books, and pamphlets, was produced. As well as providing evidence of the atrocities, many inmates wrote about pre-war topics, helping them to transport their minds away from the nightmare of their situation.

The very existence of the camp was a smokescreen to explain away the deportations of elderly Jews, who could not very well be said to be working in labour camps. Instead, the ghetto was described along the lines of a retirement spa town for the regime's undesirables. At one stage, parts of the ghetto were beautified for a propaganda film entitled *Theresienstadt: A Documentary Film from the Jewish Settlement Area*, also known as, *The Führer Gives a City to the Jews*, directed by the Jewish filmmaker Kurt Gerron, who was deported to Auschwitz and murdered after the film was made, along with most of those featured.

The first thing new arrivals such as the Götz women would have noted were the cramped conditions. Most people were crammed into converted barracks of sixty to eighty prisoners, and forced to sleep in triple decker wooden bunks, sometimes with several people sharing each bunk. Others slept wherever they could, including in attics, cellars and hallways.

Although responsibility for the ghetto was given to the Gestapo, Adolf Eichmann and the Prague Office for Jewish Emigration, day-to-day administration was handled by the Theresienstadt Jewish Council, led by chairman Jacob Edelstein. Corruption and abuse of power was rife. Therefore, those with connections often managed to obtain their own cubbyholes, while prominent folk whose mistreatment could possibly provoke anger back in Germany or abroad usually received better quarters. Connections also helped inmates to obtain more food, a scarcity in the ghetto. Meals, offered three times a day, consisted usually of potato or lentil soup, with bread, and possibly a slice of salami or meat, with coffee. It was technically possible to receive food parcels from those on the outside, but assuming such friends continued to survive long enough to send the parcels, these gifts had to make it past the guards and other inmates in a position to steal them. And while there was ostensibly running water in the ghetto, it was usually broken.

Unsurprisingly, many of the inmates who died inside Theresienstadt were claimed by starvation or illnesses caused by lack of food, combined with poor sanitation. Although there was a hospital within the ghetto, it suffered from a lack of medicine and primitive conditions. In 1942 alone, 15,891 people died — half of the ghetto's population.

One young inmate — Inge Auerbacher — later recalled: "Conditions in the camp were harsh. Potatoes were as valuable as diamonds. I was hungry, scared and sick most of the time. For my eighth birthday, my parents gave me a tiny potato cake with a hint of sugar; for my ninth birthday, an outfit sewn from rags for my doll; and for my tenth birthday, a poem written by my mother."

The ghetto was visited by the Danish Red Cross in October 1943, ironically following the deportation there of some 476 Danish Jews, a transport in which Hans Götz might well have found himself, had he not fled to Sweden. The visit was allowed by the Nazis following pressure from the Danish government, and they took the opportunity to present Theresienstadt as a 'model' ghetto, shipping out some 7,503 Jews to reduce overcrowding, holding them in a 'family camp' at Auschwitz, where the Red Cross could visit them if requested. Officials declined to do so, and they were all murdered once their purpose had been served.

Back in Theresienstadt, the Nazis arranged for buildings along the inspection route to be painted. Fake stores, a coffee house, bank, school, kindergartens and the like were opened and flower gardens were planted throughout the ghetto. The visitors could watch a football match, as well as take part in cultural activities, including lectures. The prisoners they met were closely instructed in what to say.

Despite the desperate conditions, the Götz family could still write to friends and relatives, and receive parcels. Elsbet even found time to fall in love and get married. In September 1943, the charming, well-loved and well-read Elsbet Götz wed a fifty-two-year-old doctor from Cologne, named Wilhelm Dreyer, who spent his time in camp caring for men injured fighting for Germany in World War One. Despite the age difference, they would have made a striking and formidable couple. But their fate was out of their hands. They were both taken to Auschwitz on October 19, 1944. We know this because another victim, Philipp Manes, wrote in his diary about the preparations for this transport: "Many friends are lined up. [...] Dr. Dreyer with his famous wife. He was in charge War-disabled department exemplary."[15]

Neither Elsbet nor Wilhelm survived the war, and were probably murdered in the gas chambers shortly after arrival at the concentration camp. Hans' mother Agnes, who had originally planned to follow her son to Denmark, once money was raised from the sale of the house, died in the ghetto's hospital on June 11, 1944. Of the three Götz women sent to the ghetto, only her elderly sister Dorothea survived, albeit with a broken leg. At the age of 71, she was freed by the Soviets in May 1945.

While the Götz women were suffering and dying at the hands of the Nazis, one erstwhile member of the family was enjoying a very different lifestyle. It was about the time of the divorce that Anja became unwell and underwent a series of stomach operations for an ailment that dogged her for the rest of her life. During one period of recuperation, Anja was advised to travel to warmer climes. This she did by making her way to Rome with her half-Jewish son Aldo.

Hoping to both improve her health and keep her boy free from Nazi persecution, Anja remarried to an Italian nobleman. It's not clear how much Anja knew about the fate of her former in-laws or her ex-husband. But by the time Hans, Reinold, Agnes, Dorothea and Elsbet were each being put through their own personal hell at the hands of Europe's most evil men, Anja had also begun an unlikely relationship with the architect of much of their pain — head of the SS, Heinrich Himmler.

---

[5] Ulrike Sparr, online article.

[6] Ibid.

[7] Manfredi files.

[8] Ibid.

[9] Jaeger, Roland (2011). Torre zur Bucherwelt: Hamburgs Antiquariate und Auktionshauser der Zwischenkriegszeit.

[10] Ibid.

[11] Ibid.

[12] Survivors Remember Kristallnacht: Johanna (Gerechter) Neumann. https://www.youtube.com/watch?v=Z69qY5s7Yas

[13] Ibid.

[14] Theresienstadt. United States Holocaust Memorial Museum. Link: https://encyclopedia.ushmm.org/content/en/article/theresienstadt

[15] Manes, Philipp. (2009). As If It Were Life. A WWII Diary From The Theresienstadt Ghetto.

The Baron

Anja departed her adopted homeland of Germany not long after Hitler seized power in March 1933. Precisely why she left is not known. It's possible that she was personally disgusted by the rise of Nazism, or found herself unable to work as the state clamped down on journalism. Judging from Anja's later actions, one probable motive was the desire to place her then nine-year-old son Aldo outside the jurisdiction of the anti-Jewish regime. As for her choice of destination, it seems that she opted for Italy's more agreeable climate as a measure to counteract a severe illness — almost certainly tuberculosis. While Anja's full diagnosis was never directly referred to by British intelligence, she later claimed to suffer from TB of the stomach in documents filed in the 1950s.

The disease vaguely known for hundreds of years as consumption was only proven to be caused by a bacterial infection in 1882, and by Anja's time treatment was still relatively primitive. In 1921, the BCG vaccine was used for the first time in humans, but it was still being trialled for widespread use as late as 1945. In 1943, the highly effective antibiotic streptomycin was developed, but again it was only available to selected Americans in those early years, and was of little use to Anja. For most of history, fighting TB consisted of little more than advice to get warmth, rest, and good food. Other options included taking cod liver oil, vinegar massages, and inhaling hemlock or turpentine, none of which had any real effect on the microbe that caused the illness. Little had changed by the early 1930s, although certain surgeries were available.

One option was to induce a pneumothorax, or collapsed lung, achieved when air gets into the space between a lung and the chest wall. One way of doing this was through a thoracoplasty — the surgical removal of ribs. There was also the option of a lobectomy, in which a lobe of the lung was removed to prevent the infection of others. Similarly invasive methods were used for other forms of the disease, particularly in the stomach. The most popular and least invasive treatment was to spend time at a sanatorium, taking plenty of fresh air — sometimes remaining outside in all weathers — and rest.

Anja never wrote directly of her own illness or the treatment she underwent, but it's possible to gain some idea of what she might have gone through by reading the diary of an English female patient, aged thirty-two in 1944, as she endured the disease before the introduction of streptomycin therapy.[16] The woman had been coughing up "mouthfuls of blood" and was diagnosed via x-ray with TB of the right lung. The initial treatment was to visit a sanatorium for between six and nine months, separating her from her husband, Bill, and an infant son, named Mark:

> The main thing was that for 2-3 months I needed nothing but complete rest. Then a further X-ray, and if I was coming on satisfactorily, continue similarly. If not, sanatorium and collapse the lung etc. Oh God, only when I realized I could still see Bill and Mark did I let myself think what it would have been like to have been away from them for so long. Mark will walk, talk and change completely during the coming year — nearly half his small life. And as for Bill — I know that millions of wives have their husbands away, but still — husband and baby at once!

The doctors gave her two golden rules:

1/ Absolute and utter rest of mind and body — no bath, no movement except to toilet once a day, no sitting up except propped by pillows and semi-reclining, no deep breath. Lead the life of a log, in fact. Don't try, therefore, to sew, knit, or write, except as occasional relief from reading and sleeping.
2/ Eat nourishing food and have plenty of fresh air.

After nine months she was back at home and feeling relatively rested, but the disease soon returned with a vengeance:

Haemorrhage when coughed whilst sitting quietly in lounge after dinner. Went to bed but continued bleeding three to four times a day, some slight, some nasty, till a very nasty one on Friday evening. Didn't move or speak above a whisper all Saturday and managed not to have any more, though I could feel it all there.

In March 1945, nearly one year after the original diagnosis, the patient underwent surgery, an artificial pneumothorax, which she found "quite interesting" and, at first, painless thanks to the local anaesthetic. But she soon awoke "feeling awful. Chest very painful and couldn't get into a comfortable position in bed". She was bedbound for the next day and was allowed to do next to nothing, not even read. She had a "refill" twice more that week, with no further ill effects, and then ongoing procedures and rest for several months. The woman also found time to write about the treatment endured by a fellow patient, a Mrs Pratt, who had ribs removed in a thoracoplasty after undergoing various treatments for twelve years.

Happily, in 1949, the woman was told she could become pregnant again and her second baby was born in February 1950. She went on to lead an active life and died aged eighty-six from an unrelated cause. As we shall see, Anja's experience was closer in kind to that of the long-suffering Mrs Pratt. Her disease was apparently chronic and seemingly required dozens of operations from the 1930s into the late 1950s. Fortunately, by the time war broke out, Anja had found a husband who could afford to pay for the treatment she so desperately needed.

***

Filippo Manfredi de Blasiis was born in Rome on July 4, 1906, the eldest of two sons by Baron Giuseppi and his wife Maria Franciscini. The other boy, Giacomo, was born in 1911. The Manfredis were wealthy landowners from Cerignola, a small town in the south eastern province of Foggia, famous for its red wine grapes and romantic countryside. The family could trace its illustrious ancestry all the way back to the thirteenth century, although their titles were only bestowed upon them in the late nineteenth century, when Italy became a unified kingdom.[17]

As one would expect from a noble family, the Manfredi property portfolio was impressive. They had the Palazzo Manfredi, in the town of Cerignola itself. Built by Filippo's father towards the end of the nineteenth century, its neo-Gothic facade overlooked the town square and made the Venetian palace-style building a popular subject in postcards. Above a first floor balcony was a heraldic coat of arms, featuring a golden eagle, symbol of the Manfredi family. By the time war broke out, the building was estimated to be worth some three million lire.

For country living, and to maintain themselves in business, the Manfredis had the 250-hectare Santa Maria del Manzi estate, 12km from Cerignola. Boasting six olive groves, twelve almond groves, and sixty hectares of vineyards, it was worth some nine million lire. The family's 2.5m lire Parcone estate was 13km from the town and was devoted almost entirely to grain, with seven houses also on the land. The third key estate was the 850-hectare Rio Morto, about 21km from Cerignola. There, the Manfredis had 150 hectares of olive groves, two houses and livestock including horses, poultry, and pigs. It was valued at twelve million lire. The family employed about fifteen full time workers, and hired far more during harvest periods. Besides this, the family's fortune was valued at some twenty million lire, although most of this was invested in the business. On top of all this, there were other estates in the Vittorio Veneto region, which were later inherited by Giacomo.

It was a gilded life for young Filippo. He schooled at the Tasso Lyceum and later attended the University of Rome, graduating as a bachelor of law in 1928. The following year, Filippo was called up for military service and joined the school for Bersaglieri Officers at the La Marmora Barracks in Rome. After a one-month course, he was commissioned as a 2nd Lieutenant. Filippo took another course five years later, and although he didn't complete it due to ill health, he was promoted to Lieutenant and later achieved the rank of Captain. Despite all the military training, Filippo was excused from duty when war came because of his role in agriculture.

Mussolini and his National Fascist Party took power in October 1922, and at some point Baron Manfredi joined and henceforth paid his fifty lire annual membership fee. He was also once elected to the District Agricultural Federation in Puglia, a Fascist body. However, Filippo insisted that he had no real political interests and was more or less forced to become a Fascist because of his position in society. In any case, he pointed out, he was once put on Mussolini's 'Black List' and only saved from death because of this same "reputation and standing". In his defence, it's well-known that most army officers were royalists and only paid lip-service to Facism because it came with the territory.

Filippo planned to see the war out in relative safety, luxury and liberty. The Banco di Napoli extended him a 700,000 lire overdraft and he previously held shares in the Adriatic Electric Combine and an Italian-German boat building company, to the value of 800,000 lire, which had been liquidated. The Baron was one of the most well-connected men in the country, a friend to princes, politicians, celebrities and military men, as well as plenty of lawyers — which no doubt came in handy many years later. One of his closest acquaintances was the racing driver and engineer Enzo Ferrari. Another good friend was Prince Raimondo Lanza di Trabia, a nobleman from one of Sicily's most important families. Prince Lanza was a dashing, pencil-mustachioed bon viveur and playboy who counted Rita Hayworth among his romantic conquests and Errol Flynn, who he was said to resemble, among his close friends. He was also an Italian army officer, and Filippo's association with Lanza would one day add to his woes.

As often as he could, Filippo spent his leisure time with his friends in Rome. On one such jaunt in 1934, the Baron and his party encountered Anja Bergroth and the pair soon became lovers. Anja must have been mixing in high society — she was friends with several White Russian exiles living in Rome, as well as many Germans who moved in diplomatic, artistic and journalistic circles. Anja would have been in her early thirties and Filippo in his late twenties, both well overdue to wed. They were quite possibly head over heels in love, because it wasn't long until they were engaged, although cynics might suggest that Anja targeted Filippo because of his obvious wealth. In any case, one person who wasn't thrilled about the match was Filippo's mother, Maria, who had been a widow since 1928 and was somewhat embittered. In a mirror of Oskar Bergroth's animosity towards Judith's erstwhile older lover, Anja's prospective mother-in-law hated the fact that she was divorced and already a mother.

It was now that questions about Anja's true loyalties came into play. Unbeknown to both Filippo and Anja, Maria went to the Fascist secret police, the Organizzazione di Vigilanza Repressione dell'Antifascismo (OVRA), with a serious allegation — Anja Bergroth, the woman who wanted to marry her son, was a Russian spy. We don't know whether the denunciation was merely malicious or whether Maria had some evidence for making this potentially deadly slur. It's true that Anja had a classic occupation for spies operating in a foreign country, that of a journalist, and was well-connected to White Russian exiles, as well as many Finnish, German and Swedish nationals. But she doesn't appear to have had any Communist leanings. In fact, Anja's close friendship with the aforementioned White Russians would hardly have endeared her to the Soviet Union — unless she was being asked to spy on them. No evidence has ever emerged to suggest that this was the case, and given how close Anja later got to the Nazi leadership, the Soviets would have found it impossible not to boast about her after the war.

It seems that Maria's intervention was nothing but a work of dangerous fiction, but it led to a police investigation and Anja was questioned. Having satisfied her inquisitors, and much to Maria's chagrin, Anja converted to Catholicism and married the Baron on March

9, 1937. She was now an Italian citizen. But although Maria died three years later, the claims she made lingered around Anja like a bad smell.

After a honeymoon taking in Munich, Vienna and a tour of the Tyrol, the newlyweds lived on the Cerignola estate in apparent happiness for several years, even though the secret police continued to harbour suspicions about Anja's true loyalties. The couple took occasional jaunts to Rome, and also enjoyed taking the Baron's treasured yacht, Philly, named after Maria's nickname for her son, around the Adriatic coast. Filippo saw his brother less and less after their mother's death, because they were both busy on their estates, but he did pay him a visit in hospital over Easter 1943, where he was recovering from a broken spine.

Most of the couple's closest friends were in Rome, and few of them wanted to venture down to Cerignola, although when they did head south they often remained for a short holiday. One such visitor was a sixty-five-year-old German poet, musician and broadcaster, who was said by British intelligence to be a personal friend of Anja's. He stayed for around a month after visiting primarily for health reasons. Another visitor was Ilse von Griesheim, a German aristocrat and travel writer who turned out be an agent of the OVRA. She stayed at the Palazzo Manfredi during the winter of 1940-41, during which she had a blazing row with Anja over the bombing of London, a tactic that Anja was apparently strongly against. British spies believed that von Griesheim supplied this tidbit, and other information, to the OVRA.

They say that all roads lead to Rome, and that was the way Anja liked it. Country living in Italy's rural south east wasn't for her and she continually felt the lure of the capital city. Besides her White Russian friends, who included the exiled Prince Dimitri Galitzine as well as members of the "Messing and Canaplef" families, the city was also home to Anja's "uncle," the Finnish ambassador Onni Talas, whose wife, Aina Lemmikki, was a travel writer and the Rome correspondent for the New Finland newspaper. Like many Finns, Talas had at one point in the 1890s changed his name because the original, Gratschoff, was too Russian. However, it has not been possible to establish where he might fit, if at all, into Anja's family tree.

As well as these characters, Anja was also very well known among Germans living in the city — including Nazis. Under later interrogation, Filippo Manfredi supplied the names of many of his wife's associates. These included Swedish and Finnish diplomats, and friends in Germany and Switzerland, such as a Dr Spengler, a businessman who held a stake in plants producing gas generators for cars, which were sold to the Italian government. He would prove to play an important role in Anja's recruitment by the Nazis. Manfredi's list of Anja's friends also included several Jews and the "Goetz family", although how well they would by then have regarded Anja in return is open to speculation. Filippo probably knew nothing of their travails.

The Baron and his wife rented a house at 44 Piazza Farnese from a German named Molier, who was officially attached to the German embassy's press section, but was more likely than not a member of the Nazi foreign intelligence service, the Ausland-SD, or Amt VI of the RSHA. Germany was officially banned from conducting espionage activities inside Italy at the time, but nevertheless many spies were undercover in Rome posing as journalists or press officers. Filippo later told MI5 how Molier "had no illusions" about the future of the Nazi movement, pointing out that Allied bombing raids had destroyed many German factories, putting them at least four to five months behind. But as Manfredi was not particularly sympathetic to the Nazi cause, this could well have been an attempt by Molier to gain his confidence.

Another good friend of Anja's was a German naval captain named Sembt, based at headquarters in Rome. Previously, he had lived in Bremen with his wife and children. Filippo found Sembt to be easy company, primarily because the German was himself a keen yachtsman and was very interested in Manfredi's shipyard and boat building interests, supposedly with a view to moving into a similar business himself after the war. Sembt and Filippo even planned to undertake a sailing tour together once hostilities ended. It was Sembt who would go on to make the introduction to the couple's most important German wartime friend, a Nazi named Koehler, introduced to Filippo as a lieutenant in the Colonial Police, recently returned from Africa. Whether or not Molier and Sembt were spies tasked with grooming the Baron and his wife is open to speculation, but Koehler most certainly was.

Koehler's real identity was Hauptsturmführer Gerhard Koehler, and he would become the point man as Filippo endeavored to have Anja's son 'Aryanised'. This involved repeated trips to the German embassy, where Filippo also became friendly with Enno Emil von Rintelen, the German military attaché in Rome and the younger brother of the famous World War One saboteur Captain Franz von Rintelen.

Of all Anja's friends, probably the most important to her personally was Dr Janos Oskar Plesch, a Hungarian Jew exiled in London. Plesch was an enigmatic physician who counted Albert Einstein among his close friends and as one of his many celebrity patients, who also included Marlene Dietrich and Count Grandi, the Italian fascist minister. Plesch fled his Berlin home after the Nazis seized power and opened up a practice in London's Harley Street. Plesch was an outspoken anti-Nazi, branding Hitler a "latrine statesman" and "a case of maniac depressive lunacy, and not even an interesting one". Plesch loved to recount an evening he spent with the German dramatist Gerhart Hauptmann during which an opportunity arose to mock the Führer's slavish devotees:

> In the course of the conversation the Nazis and their leader, Adolf Hitler, cropped up, and I asked Hauptmann whether he knew anything about the fellow. He did not, it appeared, and he turned to the company in general for information. No one seemed to know much about him or the aims of his movement, but [WWI Field Marshal Hans] von Seeckt, as always, had a joke ready. A peasant had a donkey which fell sick. He called in the vet, but the vet could do nothing, and the donkey still lay motionless on the floor of its stable. Other vets had no greater success, until finally, in desperation, the peasant called in a quack, who bent down and whispered something into the donkey's ear, whereupon the brute sprang to its feet at once. When the admiring peasant asked the quack how he had obtained such speedy results, the quack replied: 'Simple. I just whispered 'Heil Hitler'. Every donkey jumps up then.'[18]

Plesch was also an expert on tuberculosis, although he did give credence to the quack theory that garlic could be a possible method of treatment.

Plesch did not mention Anja in his autobiography, but he did write of his experiences of living in Finland during the 1920s following the revolt against the Soviets:

> The Finns are a peasant people. Even under Russian political dominance their teachers were still the Swedes, and their literary language was Swedish, as that of the Hungarians was German. It was these two languages respectively which were their keys to the world of scientific knowledge. But gratitude amongst nations is like gratitude amongst individuals; it is an embarrassing matter. Neither Finns nor Hungarians are prepared to forgive their benefactors. Whilst I was in Finland the hateful atmosphere of national chauvinism was particularly irritating. As far as the nationalistic rulers of Finland could manage it, every trace of the country's Swedish past, including place and street names, was being erased. Nationalism dominated the school curricula; Swedish professors were banished from the capital into lonely country places; Finnish text-books were hurriedly printed in great numbers to replace the old-established Swedish ones; and the name of the capital was changed from Helsingfors to Helsinki, and so on.

Anja visited Plesch in London on at least two occasions, once in 1938 and again in the Spring of 1939, when he was apparently of "great assistance" with her stomach problems.[19] This might explain her opposition to the bombing of Britain's capital city. While on one of these trips Anja also met with a sixty-five-year-old British woman who owned a property in Rome, which she had rented to Baron Manfredi in the past, and which she sold in 1938. This woman was named only as "Bergarsia" in Manfredi's British intelligence reports. She had also visited the couple in Cerignola, and early in the war had tried sending two telegrams via the Red Cross, to which the Manfredis were unable to reply. Her full identity is unknown.

Anja's trips to England left her greatly rejuvenated, but they also marked a deterioration in her relationship with her husband. After her return from London in early 1939, Anja based herself primarily in Rome, while Filippo remained on the estate in Cerignola. Anja's son Aldo spent most of his time with the Baron, where "only under constant supervision was it possible to make him study," British spies later wrote. In late 1940, Aldo, described in the files as a "boy of undeveloped intelligence", was sent to the Mare e Monte Institute near Rapallo, a small town near Milan on the Italian Riviera.

What was behind Anja's decision not to return to Cerignola? One explanation is that she had been asked to spy for the Allies, and would be more use in Rome than in rural Italy. There is no evidence that Janos Plesch was involved in espionage, although the Baron's MI5 file notes that: "The name Plesch appears on Security Service files". Anja could have met anybody in London, including Soviet operatives. As we shall see, Anja soon came under renewed suspicion by the Germans. But the much more likely explanation for the move had to do with Aldo's safety.

Under Fascist rule in Italy, Jews faced relatively little persecution, compared with Nazi Germany. In fact, in a country where Jews had long served in the upper ranks of the political classes, including as senators and a Prime Minister in 1910, many Jews in public life had embraced Mussolini's brand of Fascism. That changed in 1938, when the Duce introduced the Hitler-appeasing Italian Racial Laws, which saw Jews excluded from almost all areas of civic life, and stripped of their property, employment and other civil rights. Still, the murders, atrocities and deportations did not begin until Germany occupied the country in September 1943, as we shall see. But Anja probably saw the writing on the wall.

Both Anja and her husband were committed to having Aldo naturalized Italian, but the only way they could do so was to prove that he was not Jewish. Anja swore an oath that the child was Filippo's and that he had been born before her marriage to Hans Götz. Of course, there was no proof that this was true, and it seemed a highly unlikely scenario. A blood test was required to prove the paternity and the Manfredis successfully bribed an official to issue a fake certificate at a cost of 10,000 lire. Another bribe was paid to issue a fake birth certificate.

Armed with these documents, the Manfredis prepared an application for naturalisation. This could only be done through the German embassy in Rome, and Filippo therefore took it upon himself to befriend the spy

Koehler. It's not known whether the Baron paid a cash bribe to his new German friend, but British spies later noted that Manfredi "took care to see he was well victualled from the Cerignola estate". It was probably to further ingratiate herself with as many influential Nazis as possible that Anja decided to remain in close proximity to the German embassy. Over the following years, Anja visited her son in Rapallo once in 1941 and again in 1942, on both occasions staying for about three weeks. It appears that from her point of view, his interests were best served by her presence in the capital.

There is, of course, a further alternative explanation — Anja simply loved life in Rome. Baron Manfredi disagreed strongly with her choice of friends there, particularly because she was still under suspicion by the OVRA. In 1940, Anja was once again questioned by the secret police. As British intelligence put it:

> Up to this period she had spent much time on the Cerignola estates owned by her husband, but the life in Rome appealed to her, her interest in Manfredi flagged, and so they gradually separated. Her continual association with foreigners brought about the first disagreement between the Baron and the Baroness. He describes her as being a most intellectually able and forceful woman, which made it increasingly difficult to live with her.

Anja's insistence on living a life of intrigue must have seemed bizarre to the Baron, given the political and social capital he was expending in trying to help with her son. As a result, Filippo visited his wife in Rome less often and instead turned south to Bari for his weekend breaks, often staying at the Hotel Delle Nazioni. He spent much time there with a Signora D'Amati, a married woman and mother, whose husband was an officer in the Italian Army away on active service.

In 1941, the Italian police ordered Anja to leave the country, but Filippo was able to exploit his friendship with the head of the police, Carmine Senise, and succeeded in having the charges discontinued. It was through another friend, Count Riceschi, that he learned for the first time how the suspicions surrounding Anja had originated with his late mother. However, in 1942, Anja was again told her presence in Italy was no longer desired. This time, she sensed, there would be no talking her way out of it. Anja sent an urgent telegram to her husband and he dashed to Rome to once again plead with his old friend Senise.

The Baron was told that even though the order was largely based on the old accusations from his mother, they were now supported by extra reports from OVRA agents, and Anja's continued associations with foreigners had done nothing to alleviate suspicions. Manfredi turned to Onni Talas, Anja's supposed uncle, and asked him to contact Von Rintelen. In turn, the German appealed to the German ambassador, who agreed to guarantee Anja's good character. Faced with the prospect of a diplomatic row, the Italian authorities relented, suspending Anja's expulsion order.

Despite the reprieve, Senise suggested Anja should leave the country on holiday, until the affair had blown over. Anja accepted, and traveled to Finland, where, according to the story Manfredi later told his British interrogators, she stayed with her parents. This was, of course, impossible, but perhaps she stayed with other family members, or something was lost in translation. In any case, Anja also saw her sister Judith, who was by then a widow, and stayed for a while in Sweden with a cousin from the Winter clan.

When Anja returned to Italy, she found herself still under suspicion. Filippo decided to move her to Merano, in the South Tyrol, and then Milan. This would keep her away from her dodgy friends in Rome. But in Milan, Anja contracted serious lung problems, and was placed in hospital in a critical condition for almost a month. Even during this period, Anja was being kept under unsubtle police observation. Filippo again decided to call on his extensive web of contacts. Another friend, Pescolato, the Under Secretary of Agriculture, was asked to look into what the Baron insisted was the unwarranted harassment of his wife. The politician was able to confirm that OVRA was behind it. Manfredi then turned to a childhood friend, Colonel De Carlo, attached to the Italian military intelligence unit, the Servizio Informazioni Militare (SIM). De Carlo agreed to smooth things over with his colleagues in the OVRA, and the harassment appeared to come to an end.

Anja had been saved from expulsion. By extension, her husband's efforts had also protected Aldo, and kept his citizenship application on track. However, Koehler at the German Embassy was stalling and had yet to sign off on the paperwork. As the situation dragged on, it must have been clear to Anja that she would need something more than her husband's charm, money and impeccable connections to ensure her son's safety. She had to do something. But her health was failing. She had no choice but to travel abroad for treatment once more. What happened next may or may not have been a coincidence. But on her return, Baroness Anja Manfredi de Blasiis would find herself with a new status, catching the country's leading Nazis on the back foot with patronage from the very highest levels of the Third Reich.

---

[16] See Hurt, Raymond.
[17] Manfredi files.
[18] See Plesch.
[19] Manfredi files, Ibid.

Himmler's Love Life

Even amongst the cabal of psychopathic killers at the top of the Nazi hierarchy, Heinrich Himmler was regarded as more than a little odd. Like many sociopaths, Himmler had a difficult relationship with his parents and a bizarre set of self-dictated rules for life that governed all of his actions, both professional and personal. He was weak-willed, boastful, cowardly, nosy, and a control freak obsessed with the occult. And while he was, in his way, devoted to his wife and children, Himmler tied himself in knots justifying life with a mistress and a second family, using the prism of the Aryan cause to portray himself in a positive light. Understanding this bizarre and abhorrent figure is crucial to evaluating what sort of relationship he might have enjoyed with Anja.

Born in October 1900 and raised in a strict Roman Catholic family, Heinrich Luitpold Himmler was a sickly and needy child. His father, Gebhard, was an authoritarian teacher who one former acquaintance described as "the kind of person who grovels to his superiors while oppressing his inferiors".[20] Gebhard had also been a private tutor to

Heinrich, the son of Prince Arnulf of Wittelsbach, a role he began three years before meeting Heinrich's mother, Anna Marie Heyder. The pair married and had their first child, also named Gebhard, in 1898. When Heinrich came along, his royal namesake Prince Heinrich, still aged only sixteen, agreed to be his godfather. The prince was later killed fighting in Romania, and the loss of such an influential friend badly hurt the family's future prospects. A third brother, Ernst, arrived in 1905. Both parents were strict. Anna was a hard practicing Catholic, while Gebhard was a pedantic rule-setter, although not cruel, and he taught the children stenography and brought them into his hobby of stamp collecting.

Heinrich fell ill with lung problems aged just two and the family feared he would contract tuberculosis. As a result, Anna took the children from the family home in Passau, where Gebhard was teaching at a grammar school, to a village in the Bavarian region of Allgäu. The family later moved back to Munich, where Heinrich became a bespectacled schoolboy with a weak chin who was not particularly popular with the other boys, who saw him as a teacher's pet. Experts have theorized that as the middle son, Himmler became desperate for attention, exaggerating bouts of illness and becoming a psychosomatic. He also played up to his father's obsessiveness by keeping a detailed diary of his activities and minutia of childhood. Such interminable entries included a record of how many times he went swimming on a family trip.

Like his future boss, Adolf Hitler, the outbreak of World War One became the defining moment of Himmler's youth. He kept an obsessive track of war events, and wrote about them in his diary, noting on one occasion aged fourteen: "If only I were old enough, I'd be out there like a shot."[21] Instead, Himmler played war games with his friends and joined the Cadet Corps. It was during this period that Himmler began to experience stomach pains, which sometimes left him incapacitated. He tried to build strength through weight training, but remained a puny specimen. After trying repeatedly to get accepted for officer training, Himmler was at last admitted to the 11th Infantry Regiment in December 1917.

Despite becoming a military man, Himmler's letters home displayed a remarkable neediness. He begged for more frequent food parcels and castigated his parents if they did not reply to him quickly enough or as frequently as he wanted — Himmler wrote to his parents daily, often complaining of the conditions. In the end, Himmler spent his entire military career in training because peace was declared before he was able to see combat. This did not stop him signing his letters "Heinrich the Soldier". In contrast, Gebhard ended the war as a lieutenant and recipient of the Iron Cross. Himmler would always maintain that his true calling was that of an officer.

After the war, Himmler drifted towards right-wing politics and studied agriculture at the Technical University of Munich, although he underappreciated how much graft was required. When he gained work experience on a farm, he found the physical labour (twelve hours a day, six days a week) too much and he was bed-ridden with a fever and later diagnosed by the family doctor with an "enlarged heart".

Despite Himmler's weedy physique, obsessive character, and increasingly virulent antisemitic views, he cultivated a wide circle of friends and spent much time engaged in parties and drinking sessions. He tried to keep up his Roman Catholic faith, although he accepted that his strident antisemitism would inevitably bring him into conflict with his religious ideals. Himmler also spent much of the time falling hopelessly in love with the girlfriend of one his closest friends, wallowing in self-pity after he was ultimately rejected. "It's hard to think of anyone more heartless than many girls are who've once loved you," he wrote on one occasion.

Himmler was socially awkward and sexually inexperienced. To compensate, he intentionally buried his emotions and sought to exercise rigorous self-discipline and formality. Himmler planned conversation strategies, made sure to carry out routine personal visits, and attached huge importance to the exchange of letters and gifts. Some historians have categorised Himmler's foibles as an attachment disorder. If it were not for his violent fantasy of taking part in revolution, Himmler would have been a comical figure. In one diary entry from 1921, Himmler wrote: "Good old mummy sends me lots of goodies." Hardly the attitude of a firebrand — although the content of his diaries in general would have very much surprised his friends.

Himmler's jottings show him to be a sex-obsessed young man with many opinions about the virtues and otherwise of the fairer sex. He made frequent notes on the appearance of women he met or simply observed from afar, writing that one had "quite a bosom" while the girlfriend of another pal was "certainly a good girl. But sexy". After escorting her home on one occasion, he wrote: "I think I could've had her."[22]

Himmler also noted having long, late night conversations with friends on topics as diverse as adultery, sexual performance, abstinence, abortion, and contraception. He wrote of keeping his own passions under control, admitting that he knew "what it's like to be lying together in pairs" where the "girls are then so far gone they no longer know what they're doing". But Himmler knew how to keep himself in check. "One could do what one wants with girls and yet one has enough to do with controlling oneself. I feel really sorry for girls." These 'close calls' with women, where Himmler insisted he had exercised self-control, were a frequent topic of conversation with his best friend, Ludwig.

Bizarrely, he even ghost wrote another friend's love letters to an eighteen-year-old sweetheart who Himmler described as "a cute, charming little thing, a virgin and good girl. It would be a great shame if this girl got into the wrong hands." His view on the girl later changed when she rejected the letters he had penned.

Himmler increasingly saw himself as a soldier of destiny, creating for himself the vision of the ideal woman and vowing to steer clear of sex until he could find one. He once described this vision to his masseur Felix Kersten, stating that she should be well bred, blue-eyed, blonde "strong" and "purposeful" — and willing to help breed a new generation of the Aryan master race. Knowledge of history, Nazi philosophy and languages were essential, and he planned to set up academies to teach them.

According to Himmler, his life was a never-ending roller-coaster of sexual frisson, where he often found himself in the company of attractive women, but with whom he declined to act. "I would need only to make the first move," he wrote of one encounter on a train. "But I can't flirt and I can't commit myself now — if I don't definitely feel this is 'the one"'. Like a boxer saving himself for the fight, Heinrich the Soldier felt he could not spare the energy before "the coming war".

One of Himmler's most revealing passages on women came after an argument with a female friend, who accused him of denigrating her sex. He wrote in 1922:

A woman is loved by a proper man in three ways — As a beloved child who has to be told off and also perhaps punished because it is unreasonable, who is protected and cared for because it is delicate and weak and it is so much loved. Then as a wife and as a loyal and understanding comrade, who helps one with the battles of life, standing faithfully at one's side without restricting her husband and his intellect and constraining them. And as a goddess whose feet one must kiss, who through her feminine wisdom and childlike purity and sanctity gives one strength to endure in the hardest struggles and at moments of contemplation gives one something of the divine.[23]

At the same time, Himmler was becoming increasingly antisemitic, and his diary was littered with references to Jews and the "Jewish Question." He also began to describe himself as a "true Aryan". Himmler frequently attended right-wing public meetings and marches, and met Ernst Röhm, a Nazi party member, ally of Adolf Hitler and founder of the SA. Himmler joined the group's forebear, the Reichskriegsflagge, and Himmler the Ensign played the part of flag-bearer during Hitler's Beer Hall Putsch. Despite dodging a few bullets, Himmler was not arrested, and unlike Hitler remained free to continue his racist activism.

Himmler worked for the Nazi Party but moved back in with his parents and also tried his hand at journalism, penning a few political pieces, and oratory, by making speeches at Nazi meetings. He also began editing the *Kurier für Niederbayern*, a local Nazi newspaper covering Lower Bavaria.

In 1924, Himmler showed early signs of being well-suited to manage the Gestapo, when he hired a private detective to dig up dirt on his brother Gebhard's recently discarded fiancée, dumped on Himmler's insistence because she had shown too much affection towards another man. Himmler decided to go after the whole family and compiled a lengthy report on their most negative aspects.

Himmler's star ascended rapidly in right-wing circles, and he was increasingly lauded for his speeches. This led to him being appointed as the party's deputy propaganda chief, as well as its agricultural expert. The backbreaking work experience had finally paid off. As early as 1926, this role saw Himmler demand that local branches make reports on Jews living in their local areas, including those who had been baptized, in order to produce what he said was an "accurate statistical breakdown of the number of Jews in the population". The lists no doubt included the names of members of the Götz family in Hamburg.

In September 1927, Himmler became Deputy SS-Reichsführer of the Schutzstaffel (SS), the personal protection squad devoted to the security of Hitler and other senior Nazi leaders. He became SS-Reichsführer in January 1929. The rest of Himmler's career would see him look to constantly expand and consolidate his control over the muscle of the Nazi machine. As time went on, he found himself with direct control over the secret police, the Gestapo, and the Sicherheitsdienst (SD), the intelligence wing of the SS. As these various tools of state security, repression and genocide were wrapped up into the Reich Main Security Office (RSHA) Himmler found himself arguably the most powerful man in Nazi Germany. But despite being incredibly busy with his insidious workload, Himmler still found time to chase the perfect example of German womanhood.

Himmler enjoyed writing in his diary about the sexual tension he claimed to encounter during fleeting meetings with women. Usually, they ended with the lament that he was either too dedicated to his soldiery life to bring the relationship to fruition, or that the lady in question was simply unsuitable. That was not the case with Margarete Boden, who he met in September 1927, probably in the town of Sulzbach, where Himmler was visiting during one of his many speaking tours. Margarete was a nurse, which played well with Himmler's view of what an ideal woman should be, and she was also virulently antisemitic, a bonus. The pair wrote to each other frequently.

Margarete, seven years Himmler's senior, was a motherly figure, who pandered to Himmler's neediness and sympathized with every whinge and moan. "Oh no, do you really have to speak 20 times in these 20 meetings," she wrote. "It would be awful. And you've got to go on doing this till Christmas." But Margerete was no meek creature — she gave as good as she got. When Himmler expressed his disappointment in the less than emotional content of one letter, Margarete replied, "Frankly, I thought you would be pleased at getting two letters in such a short space of time." On another occasion, she wrote of her mistrust in men. "I have lost faith in humanity," she wrote. "Above all in men's honesty and sincerity in their relations with women."

The pair met in Berlin that December and their subsequent letters could be interpreted as a sign that Himmler had abandoned his pledge to remain celibate. Margerete began to address him as "My dear, beloved" or "Heini," the name he had been given as a child. "What shall we call the 'bigger' boy now?" she asked. In his letters, Himmler allowed all of his insecurities to flow, inviting Margerete to soothe him. There was his fear of big cities ("You needn't be frightened. I shall do my very best to protect you," she replied). His stomach problems, which Himmler himself said were psychosomatic and brought on by efforts to maintain self-discipline and control, in other words, to remain "good and decent," were a frequent topic of conversation. Himmler's greatest complex revolved around his weak chin, which he tried to cover up with his hands in an official portrait. "Why have you got your hand in front of your face," Margarete wrote, "did you want to cover up your chin?" Himmler also tied himself in emotional knots, doubting at first that his girlfriend's feelings for him were strong enough, then questioning whether he wrote to her too much. "Love without pain and worry is something I can't imagine," she wrote back on one occasion.

Margarete showed growing concern over Himmler's exacting work schedule and the direction the Nazi movement was taking. "Why do you reach for the dagger in such a bloodthirsty way?" she asked. "Being a conservative is after all a nice thing to be." And in another she wrote, "I'm sure you're not getting any sleep anymore...and the result is that you're getting ill and wretched. I'd like to know who is getting any benefit from you then."

The pair continued to meet when they could during the early part of 1928, and then they decided to marry. Margarete set about leaving the private clinic of which she was a partner, agreeing to a 12,000 marks payout from its Jewish director. "A Jew is always a Jew!" she wrote. The couple bought a house in Waldtrudering, near Munich. Her family did not approve of the match and boycotted the wedding. The new Mr and Mrs Himmler initially supplemented his meagre Nazi Party salary by breeding dogs and raising other animals, including pigs and chickens, but the enterprise didn't go well and the couple's finances were strained.

In August, Margarete gave birth to their only child, a daughter named Gudrun. The Himmlers also took in the son of a dead SS man, Gerhard, who Margarete struggled to control, calling him a "criminal type" and complaining that he stole and was "an appalling liar". Himmler tried to discipline the boy by beating him with a riding crop, and Margarete tried to give him back to his mother, but she wouldn't take him without a substantial bribe. Instead, Gerhard was shunted off to a boarding school, where he became the victim of bullies.

Himmler and his wife took a rare holiday together in Italy during the Autumn of 1937. It was the only real holiday the couple ever had and Margarete kept a diary. The pair visited all the sights of Rome, including the Colosseum, the Vatican and the Forum. "Thanks to the kindness of the police we were able to go for a drive in the Vatican park in our car with the SS pennant," Margarete wrote. Baron Manfredi's great friend Carmine Senise was deputy chief of police in Rome at the time, and no doubt any socialising the Himmlers undertook in Rome would have brought them into the orbit of further mutual friends. Although only a coincidence, this probably provided a talking point when Himmler met Anja many years later. On a similar note, Himmler's translator on the trip, Eugen Dollman, would later betray the Third Reich in a plot hatched in part by Anja's SD handler.

Although Himmler developed a "stomach upset" on the trip, the couple went on to Naples and Pompeii, where they were both very excited by the discovery of "mosaic floors with a swastika". They then went to Cosenza in Calabria and to Taormina in Sicily for a two week spell of rest and relaxation. The sojourn later took them to Libya, where Margarete wrote of the Jewish quarter, "Awfully dirty and the smell! The Arabs are much cleaner." The holiday ended back in Rome, where the Himmlers had dinner with the German ambassador to the Vatican.

By now, the Himmlers were living in grand style and owned several properties, including a lakeside house in Tegernsee, their primary residence, as well as a fourteen-room townhouse in Berlin, provided free-of-charge by the state as Himmler's official residence. The Lake Tegern chalet was equally splendid, with armed SS guards, a private dock, land for animals including pigs and sheep, a croquet meadow and a fishpond. Himmler rarely got to enjoy it, visiting just six times during 1935. Margarete resented Himmler's commitment to his work over his family. Writing in her diary, she said, "In spite of the happiness marriage brings, I have had to do without many things in my marriage for H is almost never there and his life is all work."

Margarete increasingly took her frustrations out on the long-suffering domestic staff. "Why are these people not put under lock and key and made to work until they die? Sometimes I wonder if I live with human beings or not." Margarete wanted to do her part in the war and signed up with the German Red Cross, becoming a district hospital supervisor and undertaking many trips to the occupied territories. The organization was little more than an SS front and was run by Himmler's crony, Dr Ernst-Robert Grawitz. Writing of a trip to Poland in March 1940, she said: "This Jewish rabble, Polacks, most of them don't look like human beings and the dirt is indescribable." And on a trip to Alsace, she added: "Very poor population. Sloping foreheads."

Soon after her return to Berlin, Himmler informed his wife about the affair.

Margarete was a figure of fun for the other Nazi wives, in particular Lina Heydrich. Older than most and an outsider with awkward social skills to match her husband's, Margarete was a victim of bullying. Lina Heydrich mocked Margarete's fuller figure, once writing "50 size knickers, that's all there was to her," and also describing her as a "narrow minded, humourless blonde female" who was "always worrying about protocol". Another leading Nazi spouse, Henriette Hoffman, agreed. She called Margarete "a small bad-tempered woman who seemed born to be unhappy," while others shared Lina's view that Mrs Himmler "ruled her husband and twisted him round her little finger". British Hitler fan girl Unity Mitford was said to laugh openly about Margarete.[24]

Margarete did not take the insults lying down. After complaining bitterly to her husband, Himmler asked another SS wife, Frieda Wolff, to have a quiet word with Lina Heydrich. When that failed, he suggested Heydrich should order his wife to shut up or divorce her. When Lina next met Himmler at a garden party, she made a show of remaining utterly silent and donned a mournful expression, until Himmler felt obliged to ask if she was alright. He couldn't summon the courage to confront her and she later wrote that it was "typical Himmler, on paper he ordered us to divorce, but when face to face with me, his courage left him". Amid all the animosity, there were some who had sympathy for Himmler's wife, and suggested she suffered from shell shock incurred during World War One. Margarete tried to combat her weight problems by playing Himmler's favourite sport, tennis, but she didn't take to it and soon gave up.

Tensions between Margarete and Lina Heydrich boiled over at the Nuremberg party rally of 1938, where Margerete tried to impose a timetable of events for the wives to follow. The other women, led by Lina, said Margarete was a killjoy and party pooper and they ignored her plans, sparking a furious rebuke from Margarete. Lina complained to her husband, who dutifully passed on the gripe to an indifferent Himmler.

Margarete's woes increased over Christmas, when she found herself laid up ill in bed. She spent New Year's Eve horribly unwell, and complained that the "maid situation is catastrophic. What I have to put up with is unbearable". In January, she checked into the SS-run sanatorium in Hohenlychen, just north of Berlin. Himmler did manage to visit but, as always, he was too busy to stay for long.

As the power of the Nazis expanded, Himmler's SS became increasingly cult-like, with his warped mind alone setting the parameters of morality where its members were concerned. This not only legitimized the task of systematic mass murder, in which the SS was primarily engaged, but it seeped fully into the private lives of his men.

One of Himmler's core obsessions was Aryan procreation — he wanted young German men and women to marry early and have lots of children (where they could afford to do so; his own young SS men were forbidden to wed too early in life), but children born out of wedlock were also acceptable. Indeed, with the aim of producing up to 300 children from each Verfugungstruppe battalion, Himmler resolved "to do all I can to raise our SS men's illegitimate, in most cases highly talented, children of good race and make them soldiers and officers or, alternatively, superior wives for our nation".

To this end, Himmler set up the Lebensborn association in 1935, which provided secure accommodation for single mothers to give birth, in secret if necessary, while the homes were also available to SS wives. In many cases, the babies became the wards of the association. Each mother was only to be accepted after being examined by an SS doctor, to ensure racial purity. It was funded by a levy on SS members, with childless members forced to pay the most, while any with four or more children were spared the charge. Himmler's liberal views on extramarital affairs and illegitimate children coincided with his own extra-marital affair with his secretary.

Hedwig Potthast started work as Himmler's private secretary in 1936, aged twenty-three. She had worked her way up through the ranks of the Gestapo press department in Berlin, after graduating university with a degree in English. She was a well-regarded young woman nicknamed Bunny on account of her friendly, outgoing personality and love of sports, including gymnastics and rowing. The younger, sportier, more confident Hedwig was a direct contrast with Himmler's older and physically ailing wife. The pair confessed their love for one another two years later, before consummating their relationship in 1940.

Himmler must have faced a pressing internal need to justify the relationship to himself, formerly a good Catholic boy who lived his life by the creed of self-restraint, and the affair was no doubt the driving force behind his policy pronouncements. As well as illegitimate children,

Himmler was also open to divorce, so long as the divorcing party was "decent" and "chivalrous". But Himmler's interest in Germanic history had opened his eyes to a far superior concept — second marriage. He announced that SS members could find themselves a second wife, provided they intended to have children with the other woman.

The SS-Reichsführer thought it would be inconsiderate to his wife to get a divorce, or at least that was the cowardly excuse he offered. Instead, the only "honourable" path forward, he decided, was to make Hedwig his second wife and start a new family. Naturally, Himmler only wanted to tell Margarete of his other life after children had been born. But news of the affair soon leaked out and one of the first to know was Lina Heydrich. She approved of Hedwig and called her "an intelligent woman characterised by warm-heartedness", unlike Margarete, who she regarded as "a narrow-minded petit-bourgeois". According to Lina, Himmler's new lover helped the insecure SS chief "achieve true stature". Another member of the Nazi wives set who knew about the affair was Gerda Bormann. She grew close to Hedwig and the pair exchanged letters and photographs.

Hedwig quit her job in early 1941 and the next year she gave birth to a son, Helge, at the same SS clinic where Himmler's wife had been treated years earlier. Hedwig, whose parents had disowned her, was moved to a charming woodland cottage in the Mecklenburg forest, just five miles from Ravensbruck concentration camp. Himmler then installed her at a property in the Alpine resort of Berchtesgaden. Martin Bormann loaned Himmler the money from party funds to purchase this secret home for his mistress. According to his confidante, the spy chief Walter Schellenberg, Himmler felt he'd been "taken advantage of" in respect to the interest rate.[25]

Berchtesgaden was, of course, a Nazi stronghold and Hitler had built his Kehlsteinhaus, the Eagle's Nest, overlooking the town, but more importantly it was close to the Berghof, Hitler's main headquarters. While Hitler rarely ventured down to the market town (the complex was equipped with its own amenities), the town did have an airstrip for his own personal use, and a railway station. Margarete rarely visited the Berghof, because she was not part of the 'in' crowd. It meant that whenever Himmler was summoned to meet with the Führer, he would be able to discreetly check in on his (second) wife and kids.

Despite the idyllic setting, there was a horror stored in the cottage's attic — Hedwig marveled at the chair with a seat made from a human pelvis and human legs and feet. Martin Bormann's son, also named Martin, later recalled how Hedwig was able to "clinically and medically explain how it was made". Hedwig also kept copies of Mein Kampf bound with the skin of former Dachau inmates and showed the items off to his mother, Gerda, but the Bormanns were "shocked and petrified" by the macabre mementos.

In this respect Hedwig had another thing in common with Margarete, who had also made use of prisoners held at Dachau. In August 1944, a team of slave labourers was used to build a bomb shelter at her Tegernsee home. She complained about their quality. And if there was any doubt about Margerete's complicity in the horrors of the Holocaust, in July 1941 she and Gudrun were given a tour of the large herb and spice gardens Himmler had created at the concentration camp, using the slave labour of some 1,000 prisoners.

In any case, the location of Himmler's love nest meant that there was a good 120 miles between the homes of the two wives. Himmler and Hedwig had their second child, Nanette-Dorothea, on July 3, 1944, again at the SS clinic. Himmler was unable to attend, because he was at a party at the Berghof for the marriage of Eva Braun's younger sister to an SS officer, Hermann Fegelein.

But as early as February 1941, the cat was out of the bag and Margarete knew all about Hedwig Potthast. Writing of an acquaintance's humiliation after her husband got another woman pregnant, but in a line that could easily have been self-referential, she said: "Men think of doing that only when they're rich and successful. If not, their not-so-young wives have to feed them, help them, or stick it out with them. What times we live in!" Later, she was more direct. Writing of an imminent visit from Himmler, she said: "Now Heini's coming there'll be a lot of trouble. One can't look forward to anything. I will and must put up with it all for the sake of my child."

Himmler still had a good relationship with Gudrun, who he called Püppi. He phoned at least three times a week and exchanged letters with her frequently. Margarete never considered divorce, although there is no doubt that she hated the humiliating situation. On one occasion she wrote: "So much sadness makes it hard to be alone...so in the evenings I mostly play Solitaire and read a little". She also wrote of trying to protect Gudrun from the evils of men and the "bitter life" they inflict on women. In another note, she lamented: "Surrounded by lies and betrayal. I can't bear it anymore, I am always alone."

Himmler was an insecure, weak-willed mummy's boy who was more than willing to change his policy pronouncements to suit developments in his private life. He had no problem cheating on his wife, was prone to a romantic world view, and was seducible by any woman who could effectively mirror his concerns and obsessions. Himmler also happened to be in a position of immense power within the Nazi regime. These characteristics made him a perfect target for agents of influence — and for those looking to further their own interests.

---

[20] Longerich, p.12.
[21] Longerich, p.22.
[22] Longerich, Ibid.
[23] Longerich, p.56.
[24] Wyllie, p.114-116.
[25] See Schellenberg (book), p.313.

A Fainting Fit

While Heinrich Himmler was juggling his demanding career as a mass murdering bureaucrat with the tricky task of handling both a wife and mistress, Baroness Anja Manfredi de Blasiis was trying to combine her active social life in Italy with managing her extremely poor health. Previously, Anja had been able to find pleasure in the midst of even her most debilitating bouts of sickness, for example by visiting the enigmatic Dr Plesch in London, or her family back in Finland. By early 1943 there was still an inextricable link between her social activities and her healthcare, but the war blazing across Europe was making the good life increasingly hard to come by.

That year, Anja had initially wanted to travel to a clinic in Switzerland, but her papers had not been in order in time for the trip. It was the Manfredi family friend Dr Spengler who — at least as far as Filippo was able to ascertain — was the one who advised Anja to go Germany for treatment instead.[26] Manfredi told his MI5 interrogators how Spengler recommended a nursing home in Neuheim, near Nuremburg, close to where his family lived.

Anja stayed at the facility for most of February and March, but made little improvement. While there, she continued to make inquiries about the status of Aldo's naturalisation back in Italy, but nothing was happening and she decided not to press the matter because the police had taken an interest in the situation. Instead of returning home, Anja decided instead to recuperate in the Bavarian Alps resort of Berchtesgaden, home to Himmler's mistress Hedwig Potthast.

Anja's choice of Berchtesgaden proved to be life-changing, but it raises questions as to her true motives for going there. On the one hand, it made perfect sense, because of the clean air and high altitude, thought to be important for treating tuberculosis. On the other, it was a well-known Nazi stronghold and the home of Adolf Hitler. It was no secret that he lived in nearby Obersalzburg — Hitler's sprawling Berghof complex had taken years to complete and the construction of the Eagle's Nest, on the Kehlstein, created an awful din that washed over the region for months. If an intelligence organisation wanted someone to inveigle their way into Nazi high society, there were few better places to be during wartime than Berchtesgaden. The town was full of Nazis, and when Hitler was there, which was often, so too were many senior members of the regime. There is no evidence that Anja was asked to go to Berchtesgaden by a third party, nor that she had any ulterior motive in staying there, but if the choice of venue was a coincidence, then it was not to be the last.

Anja evidently found social company in the town and enjoyed dining out. One night in April 1943 she happened to be in a restaurant when Heinrich Himmler also came in to dine. We don't know who he was with, but he was more likely in the company of SS cronies than with his mistress, who would probably have been at home with their son. Did Anja see and recognise the SS-Reichsführer during the course of her meal? It's tempting to believe that their eyes met once or twice during the course of the evening, as Anja gossiped with her friends about acquaintances back in Rome, while Himmler held forth on one of his wacky favourite subjects, such as the occult or what he saw as the unfair treatment of German witches during the Middle Ages.[27]

In any case, as Anja got up to leave she appeared to faint. Himmler — no doubt to the surprise of those present — rushed over to help and offered the use of his official car to take her home. This was how Anja related the story to her husband, and how he subsequently described the incident to British intelligence. It was also backed up, as we shall see, by a captured SS man, Klaus Hügel, who later had dealings with Anja.

Anja's meeting with Himmler was further corroborated in the captured diaries of Nazi spymaster Guido Zimmer, although he mentioned her fainting in a hotel room in front of a mirror. This detail was gleaned from inquiries made to a "Dr Scheidt", who said Anja had subsequently "painted her relationship with [Himmler] in a harmless way".[28] Another partial account of the meeting, which has survived in the declassified files of other senior Nazis based in Italy, tells the story slightly differently. It was said that Anja had been invited to dine privately with Himmler in his room at the Grand Hotel, which is where she fainted. This account, however, appears to have come from Anja herself during interrogation by Allied forces and should be treated with the utmost caution. According to her dubious re-telling, which we will touch upon again later, Anja did not see Himmler again.[29]

Wherever Anja fainted, one can well imagine Himmler's reaction to this dramatic and unexpected scene as she crumpled to the floor. According to Anja, Himmler merely offered assistance and the use of his car. But Himmler, with his over-exaggerated sense of chivalry and obsession with interfering in the lives of others, would no doubt have rushed over personally to check on Anja's condition. He would surely have insisted on sending her a recovery gift and probably visited her personally while he was still in town. Whether or not any further intimacy took place at this stage is open to speculation. But we know that from Himmler's youthful diaries and his two year courtship of Hedwig Potthast, he did not need to jump straight into bed before taking a relationship seriously. The encounter with Anja was the sort of 'meet-cute' the young Himmler would have fantasised about — and he would likely have convinced himself that he could 'have' the Baroness whenever he wanted.

If indeed the two did spend further time getting to know one another during Anja's recuperation in Berchtesgaden, they would have found plenty in common. Both were Roman Catholic; he was lapsed, she was a non-practising convert. He had studied agriculture in his youth; Anja's husband was a farmer by profession — not to mention that her ex-husband had attended the same college as Himmler. Both had an interest in journalism, (Himmler's brother Ernst, also an SS member, was by now head of the Nazi's broadcasting organization). Most importantly, both had spent years suffering with ill health. Tuberculosis was highly stigmatized in Nazi Germany, and its carriers deemed to be of racial inferiority. As a result, thousands were forcibly sterilized or murdered. Anja, therefore, might have been very discreet about the exact nature of her illness. But that would have been perfect, because Himmler also seemed to suffer from a mystery stomach ailment for which he required the frequent use of a private masseur. And while we don't know much about Anja's political views or her feelings about the Nazi treatment of Jews — beyond her own son — if they diverged from those of Himmler, then she certainly would have kept them to herself. However, the pair almost certainly discussed their children, as evidenced by a note Himmler would later send to Anja when she was back in Italy. And as we shall see, as far as the gossips in the SS were concerned, there was little doubt that the relationship progressed to the physical side.

Whatever the facts of the case, the coincidental meeting between Anja and Himmler sounds too good to be true. We've already seen why it's highly unlikely that Anja was a Soviet spy, and it's equally improbable that she was working on behalf of the British or Americans, neither of whom seemed to know much about her at the end of the war. But there is a third, entirely plausible scenario.

Since 1939, Himmler had been in thrall to an Estonian-born Baltic German masseur with Finnish citizenship named Felix Kersten. Himmler believed that without the "magic hands" of his physical therapist he would quite literally die. But what he didn't know, and what he refused to accept despite repeated warnings from his top officials, was that Kersten was a spy. And although untrained in traditional spycraft, Kersten became a master agent of influence, mostly on behalf of the Swedish and Finnish governments.

Kersten's career is worth summarizing, as it speaks to the intrigue and double-dealing surrounding Himmler and his closest aides. Kersten had fought bravely in the German Army in Finland against the Russians, sustaining an injury in the Battle of Helsinki, and was later commissioned into the Finnish Army as a second lieutenant. He remained in Helsinki to train in medicine but later moved to Berlin, where he became a master of his craft under the tutelage of a leading Chinese masseur. When Himmler 'invited' him to become his personal, full-time therapist, Kersten discreetly appealed to Finland's ambassador, hoping to escape the country. But Finland had little power to intervene, and Kersten was told that he should take advantage of the unique opportunity and report back all the intelligence that he could. Two years later, Finland found herself fighting on the same side as the Nazis against the Soviet Union — although not technically an Axis ally, Finland styled itself a "co-belligerent".

Kersten always insisted that he was personally horrified by Nazism and in particular the extreme antisemitic opinions and genocidal plans that Himmler openly discussed with him. Accepting that he had no choice but to work for the man, he decided to set about using his position not just to report intelligence, but to act as a freelance saviour of Jews and other concentration camp prisoners. This he did by exploiting his private time with Himmler to put his case, sometimes insisting that the SS chief must ease his mental burden in order to alleviate his physical pains.

One of Kersten's early victories was talking Himmler out of a plan to deport Holland's Jews in 1941, arguing that such a monumental logistical undertaking would inevitably damage his health. Kersten later wrote that he told Himmler to "obey his orders if he wanted to be fit for work". Referring to his weak physique, he added: "If you put ten amps on a circuit made for six you are bound to blow a fuse." Kersten used every opportunity to nag the SS-Reichsführer and it seemed to pay off — one day in April 1941 Himmler telephoned Kersten to say the operation had been indefinitely postponed.

Further success stories followed. In July 1942, Kersten accompanied Himmler on a trip to Helsinki, where the SS-Reichsführer met with politicians to discuss Germany's post-war plans for ostensibly neutral Sweden. Himmler said that Sweden would be divided and Finland given the Finnish-populated north, while south and central Sweden would be incorporated into the Third Reich. The meeting did not go well, with Finland's foreign minister pointing out that such a plan would be hated by most Finns, who held Sweden in high regard. Sensing a diplomatic rift on the horizon, the malleable Himmler backtracked and said nothing had been set in stone.

Later, Kersten was able to secretly meet with the foreign minister and pass on a vital piece of intelligence — Himmler also planned to use the visit to raise the issue of rounding up, deporting and then murdering Finland's 2,500 Jews. The only way to deal with the issue would be to stall, both men agreed, so Kersten vowed to convince Himmler not to raise the subject at all, pointing out that such a policy would spark public anger and therefore would lead to an ugly confrontation with the already riled minister. Kersten succeeded in diffusing the situation and Himmler left without ever having raised the subject.

On another occasion, Kersten was able to secure the release of dozens of Jehovah's Witnesses, by allowing them to work on his estate in Germany, a move that placed him under the spotlight of the Gestapo, whose chief Heinrich Müller insisted: "One day I shall uncover this spy."

Müller was not alone in his suspicions. Himmler was forced to issue personal rebukes to both Heydrich and his then-deputy, Ernst Kaltenbrunner, telling them to leave Kersten alone. But Kersten continued in his endeavors to free people trapped in concentration camps, including many on behalf of the Dutch resistance. In August 1944, Kaltenbrunner and Müller went so far as to try and have Kersten murdered in a motorcade ambush. Himmler's close confidante, and Kaltenbrunner's enemy, Walter Schellenberg, was able to get a note to him at the last moment and Kersten's driver took an alternative route. Himmler later admonished Kaltenbrunner, warning him: "My dear

Kaltenbrunner, if anything were to happen to Kersten, not only would my life be in danger, but yours too. I fear that you would only survive Kersten by a few hours."[30]

In 1942, after the assassination of Heydrich, Kersten also began treating his former deputy, the aforementioned Schellenberg, an intellectual and ambitious young Nazi who had risen through the ranks and was still in his early thirties when Heydrich was killed. Himmler was fond of Schellenberg, who he nicknamed "Benjamin," and appointed him as his "plenipotentiary" and therefore closest advisor.[31] Schellenberg had the advantage of despising Kaltenbrunner, who was Hitler's pet. Kaltenbrunner, the spymaster later noted, was thuggish, smoked up to a hundred cigarettes a day, and began drinking habitually soon after breakfast. His teeth were so "extremely unpleasant" that Himmler ordered him to see a dentist. On another occasion, Kaltenbrunner almost "had a stroke" when he caught Schellenberg trying to discreetly pour away alcohol he'd foisted upon him.[32]

Schellenberg was a cold and calculating man who nevertheless had no particular enthusiasm for the Jewish genocide, or the war in general. He had divorced his first wife when she became too old to have children, and married another who gave him three offspring. When the delivery of the last child proved to be difficult, Kaltenbrunner had to give him a direct order to attend his wife's bedside. According to his British intelligence files, Schellenberg took no advantage of his position within the regime and lived entirely within his ration allowance, unlike many leading Nazis. British officers thought he was on the verge of malnutrition, and would have been if not for the attention of his private secretary. Still, the British assessed him as a "man who under no circumstances can be trusted".

Schellenberg later gave a colourful account of being treated by Kersten, a procedure that Himmler insisted all his appointees must go through:[33]

> I found myself confronted by Dr Kersten, a man who was rather more corpulent than the average, who had a pleasant face and a kindly manner, which is often the way with fat people. He massaged and kneaded my

stomach with his stubby fingers, and caused a certain amount of momentary pain, but I already felt better after the first treatment and after the fifth visit I found that the pain had subsided for the first time.

In fact, the relationship between Kersten and Schellenberg was more than that of doctor and patient. They were co-conspirators. Schellenberg had long wanted to succeed Heydrich, who many felt had maneuvered the weak-willed and naïve Himmler into a position of huge power and was waiting to topple him and assume his titles. Instead, upon his death Kaltenbrunner was made overall head of the RSHA and Schellenberg moved to head up the foreign intelligence branch, Amt VI, the Ausland-SD. He still, however, had ambitions to become the 'power behind the throne' and, even though Kaltenbrunner was above him in rank, Schellenberg reported directly to Himmler.

Together, Kersten and Schellenberg colluded to influence Himmler in the direction of opening talks with Britain and America, with a view to ousting Hitler and taking on the Russians. Schellenberg offered Himmler his private but official counsel in these matters, while Kersten, seemingly independently, tried to sway Himmler towards taking action for the benefit of his health.

Schellenberg recognized that Kersten was "manipulative," noting in his post-war memoirs: "During all the years of the War he was Himmler's shadow, for Himmler believed that without Kersten's treatment he would die. In the end Himmler became completely dependent upon him." But Himmler constantly vacillated, to the frustration of both men. Kersten played a further part by drafting in an astrologist, Wilhelm Wulff, to influence the superstitious and occult-obsessed Himmler with horoscopes packed full of good tidings. Wulff later wrote a rather unflattering description of Himmler, in which he described his small, mouse gray eyes, "jerky movements" and weak chin that receded "like the jaw of a shark". In his view, Himmler's tightly drawn mouth gave his face a sharp look and disguised his "basic feebleness and cruelty".[34]

In September 1943, the former Finnish prime minister and ambassador to Germany, TM Kivimakki, persuaded Himmler to allow

Kersten to move his family to Stockholm, so that his skills could be put to use treating Finnish soldiers convalescing there. Kersten was in favour with the Swedish government, thanks to his success in having a group of suspected Swedish spies released from a concentration camp. He began working closely with the Swedish foreign minister on plans to win the release of more Scandinavian prisoners. Meanwhile, with Himmler leaning towards a putsch, but still fearful of betraying the Führer, Schellenberg pursued openings with the Allies, mostly through agents of the Office of Strategic Services (OSS), a forerunner of the CIA, based in Switzerland. But as we shall see, these efforts did not bear fruit.

What was unarguably Kersten's greatest victory came in March 1945, when he succeeded in persuading Himmler not to pass on the deranged order from Hitler that all concentration camp inmates must be slaughtered lest they fall into the hands of the Allies. Furthermore, on April 20, 1945, he arranged a meeting between Himmler and Norbert Masur, a member of the World Jewish Congress in Sweden. This meeting, during which Himmler told the sickening lie that concentration camp crematoria had only been built to dispose of bodies from a typhoid epidemic, secured the release of some 7,000 Jewish women from Ravensbrück.

Kersten also played a central role in arranging talks with the Swedish nobleman Count Folke Bernadotte, which led to the so-called White Buses operation between March and May 1945, in which some 15,000, mostly Danish and Norwegian prisoners, were freed from concentration camps under cover of white buses painted with the Red Cross emblem.

Himmler's motivation throughout these deals was obviously to curry favour with the Jewish organisations and by extension whichever authority would later be convened to try the Nazis for war crimes. It was his first step in a deranged plan for self-rehabilitation, as we shall see.

After the war, the Dutch monarchy awarded Kersten the Order of Orange-Nassau and he was credited by the World Jewish Congress with saving some 60,000 Jews from death in concentration camps. Given the phenomenal success that Kersten achieved by Himmler's side, the Finnish government would surely have jumped at the chance to infiltrate another agent into the SS-Reichsführer's orbit. That brings us back to the main subject of our tale — because Anja Manfredi was eminently well-connected to the Finnish elite and could have been recruited on one of her trips back home, or in Rome by her diplomat 'uncle' Onni Talas. If she could inveigle her way into Himmler's circle, she would be able to influence him in Finland's favour — whatever the outcome of the war.

From her point of view, such a plot would have had its advantages. Anja would have been able to lobby for her son at the very top of the Nazi hierarchy, and she would also potentially get access to funds to help pay for her ongoing treatment. No documents have emerged to prove that Anja became a spy for Finland, and there is no evidence that she ever knew or met Felix Kersten socially, although it would not be surprising if their circles had overlapped. But it is the most likely alternative to the theory that her meeting with Himmler was mere coincidence.

Equally puzzling as to how and why Anja ended up encountering and apparently beguiling the SS-Reichsführer in April 1943, is the question of why Himmler seemed to put so much faith in the Finnish noblewoman after just the one meeting. As we shall see, even his most able and astute commanders could not erode his faith in her. It's worth considering Himmler's state of mind at the time of the incident with Anja, which coincided with a period of crisis for the Nazi leadership.

In January 1943, the army had found itself starving to death in the quagmire of Stalingrad. At the end of the month, hopelessly surrounded and outgunned, its leaders defied Hitler's orders to fight to the death and surrendered. It would prove to be the tipping point in the war. From this moment on, the focus of many Nazi minds (although not Hitler's) turned from how to achieve victory, and instead began to ponder how to manage inevitable defeat.

Tragically, to Himmler's twisted mind that also meant ramping up the Nazi killing machine to horrifying levels. This process had in fact begun in July 1942 when — after the assassination of Heydrich — Himmler launched Aktion Reinhard, an effort to wipe out Poland's Jews once and for all. By the summer of 1943, more than two million people had been murdered in gas chambers and by other methods at Treblinka, Sobibor and Belzec. Just a few months before the meeting with Anja, Himmler also instigated a reign of terror in occupied France.

Following the encounter in Berchtesgaden, this escalation of the genocide included, in July 1943, Himmler's announcement that northern Ukraine and occupied Russia were to be "cleared of all their population". Men, women and children were transferred to concentration camps and many agricultural areas were planted with Kok-Sagys, a rubber plant that Himmler was obsessed with cultivating in order to fulfil Germany's needs, even though it was ultimately useless (adding to his many titles and responsibilities, Himmler had himself appointed as the Reich's "special representative for plant rubber"). Anyone left behind was summarily executed as a "bandit". A similar policy would soon be enacted in occupied Italy. There then followed the persecution of Jews in Denmark during late 1943 (from which Hans Götz was forced to flee), and the subsequent mass murder of Danish officials who opposed collaboration; and another crackdown in Poland and the Czech Republic under the guise of combatting "bandits".

But at the same time that Himmler was unleashing genocide on Europe's Jewish population, he was also considering a future without Hitler, and how he would be perceived in the inevitable event that Germany would lose the war. Spurred on by Kersten and Schellenberg, Himmler was looking for a way to win the peace, and as we have seen he cynically played with the lives of captured Jews to leverage his position. In other words, Himmler was becoming desperate.

Anja would have impressed Himmler with her forceful personality, intelligence, good education and international connections. Her friendships with notable Jews in Switzerland and London would have been a distinct advantage. If Anja had offered to speak on his behalf as a harbinger of peace, Himmler would no doubt have been willing to put his resources at her disposal. And if, during the course of their time in Berchtesgaden, Anja had indeed been willing to show him physical affection, then it's hard not to imagine that Himmler would have been in thrall to her.

A Fainting Fit

In the late summer of 1943, Himmler, now with additional power and responsibility as the Reich Minister of the Interior, wrote his long-suffering wife an emotional letter, signed off "with special affection and...many kisses". It had followed a stream of presents, including flowers and sweet treats, that he sent to the villa at Lake Tegernsee. Himmler was feeling guilty about something, and it wasn't the mass murder of the Jews. That was evidenced by the notorious speech he gave on October 4, 1943, to the SS Group Leaders in Poznan:

One principle must be absolute for the SS man: we must be honest, decent, loyal, and comradely to members of our own blood and to no one else. What happens to the Russians, what happens to the Czechs, is a matter of utter indifference to me. Such good blood of our own kind as there may be among the nations we shall acquire for ourselves, if necessary by taking away the children and bringing them up among us. Whether the other peoples live in comfort or perish of hunger interests me only in so far as we need them as slaves for our Kultur. Whether or not 10,000 Russian women collapse from exhaustion while digging a tank ditch interests me only in so far as the tank ditch is completed for Germany. We shall never be rough or heartless where it is not necessary; that is clear. We Germans, who are the only people in the world who have a decent attitude to animals, will also adopt a decent attitude to these human animals, but it is a crime against our own blood to worry about them and to bring them ideals. I shall speak to you here with all frankness of a very grave matter. Among ourselves it should be mentioned quite frankly, and yet we will never speak of it publicly. I mean the evacuation of the Jews, the extermination of the Jewish people...Most of you know what it means to see a hundred corpses lying together, five hundred, or a thousand. To have stuck it out and at the same time — apart from exceptions caused by human weakness — to have remained decent fellows, that is what has made us hard. This is a page of glory in our history which has never been written and shall never be written.

These were the words of the man who — for whatever reason — Anja now agreed to work for.

***

By early May 1943, Anja's papers for travel to Switzerland had been finalised and she prepared to leave Berchtesgaden. She traveled to Zurich via Munich and checked into the Zurich University Clinic and the care of a Dr Schmidt, possibly the same doctor who later furnished Guido Zimmer with his information about the meeting with Himmler. Anja also consulted several other physicians at around the same time and as a result her bills were racking up. In order to pay for all this, she obtained a 15,000 lire loan from a wealthy Jewish friend, a Mr Seligman, who lived in Basel with his Swiss wife.

Anja had known Seligman for some years, before her marriage to Filippo, and he had previously purchased her library. When the couple visited Switzerland during their honeymoon tour, Filippo met the German and they got along famously. It's questionable as to whether Seligman would have willingly offered the cash if he had known about Anja's encounter with Himmler just a few weeks previously. In any case, the Baron repaid the loan as swiftly as he could.

Anja was joined at her hotel in Zurich by another mutual friend of the couple, Gianni Hecht, who the Manfredis had first met at an Italian health spa in 1940. When Hecht returned to Rome after a short stay, he was able to meet the Baron and apprise him of his wife's progress, which wasn't good. Given that the Hecht described in the British intelligence files by Baron Manfredi had an unusual name — with apparent Italian and Germanic ancestry — it's likely that his real identity was Gianni Hecht Lucari, an Italian movie producer with Jewish ancestry who had been born in Vienna. He was just the sort of person who came into Anja's orbit. More pertinently, he was later to serve with the British Army as an Italian intelligence liaison officer. If the two men were indeed identical, Hecht was yet another spy in Anja's life.

According to Baron Manfredi, Dr Schmidt decided that Anja needed an urgent operation. It would be her fifteenth surgery, an ordeal that had by this point cost some 32,000 lire in total. Anja was supposedly sent to Berlin for the procedure. At one point, her condition was said to be critical and the Baron made every effort to visit her, but he was denied entry on account of being an Italian officer. Of course, it's entirely possible that Anja was sent to Berlin to receive training or to meet with Himmler, or at least his advisor, Schellenberg.

During her recuperation, Anja once more visited her cousin in Sweden and also took a trip to Finland. Who she met there and what was discussed during these travels is not known. If she had indeed been asked by the Finnish government to make contact with a senior Nazi, she would have had an explosive to tale to tell of her meeting with Himmler.

Anja returned to Rome in July 1943, a critical moment in the nation's war. On July 10, the Allies invaded Sicily. Rome was bombed for the first time on July 19. Mussolini was ousted on the 25th. As soon as he was able, Baron Manfredi came to the city to see his wife. He was relieved to find her in one piece, but dismayed to find she was out on the town with her old friends, boasting loudly of her meeting with Himmler. By the time Manfredi got to her, half of Roman society had heard the tale and formed their own opinions about what had really taken place.

Colonel de Carlo, Manfredi's old friend, warned Anja to keep her mouth shut. "Himmler is a dangerous person to know," he told her, adding that she should forget all about the meeting. But Anja was never one to be told what she could and could not say. Filippo went back to Cerignola to supervise the start of the grain harvest but returned to Rome five days later. He planned to send Anja back to Switzerland, ostensibly for further treatment, but also to keep her out of trouble. If the Allies were to advance up to Rome then her story about Himmler, whatever it really meant, could be a death sentence. And it would be worse if Italian partisans got hold of her.

On August 29, Filippo called on his German contact Gerhard Koehler for a cup of coffee and a chat. The subject of the conversation was his irascible wife. Manfredi said that he would arrange a passport, while Koehler agreed to lay on transport to the Swiss border. If necessary, she could use his official car, because as a German officer he would be able to obtain petrol. The two men discussed the war. Manfredi said he must return to Cerignola, fearing what would happen to his property if and when the Allies advanced up the coast. He was also worried about his brother, and asked if Koehler would be willing to help if the time came. To this end, he gave the family addresses of Vittorio Venetto, Fossalto di Piave, and others in Venice and Pescara. Koehler said he would do what he could. Then, he added, "As you came to ask me a favour you might be able to do something for us."

"I would be willing to do anything to help Italy," was the nuanced reply Manfredi would later insist that he gave.

"Would you be willing to look after a man who is a specialist in sabotage and keep him in the country near your estate?" Koehler asked. The man, Koehler added, was not yet in Rome but he was to arrive shortly from Milan. Koehler suggested employing him as a watchman and Manfredi said this might be arranged.

Koehler believed there was plenty of time to put the plan into action. After all, he reasoned, the Allies would not be able to land on the Italian mainland until at least September 15. As Manfredi walked out of the nearly two-hour long meeting, Koehler warned him not to say anything to the Italian General Staff. Koehler trusted him. But he was wrong on two counts. Not only would the Allies land much sooner, on September 3, just five days after the conversation, but Fillipo almost immediately relayed the details of their chat to his friend Colonel de Carlo.

During a meeting at the Excelsior Hotel, the Baron told the colonel he wanted to keep everything above board with the Italian General Staff. De Carlo advised him not to do anything for Koehler and forget about the conversation. They walked out of the hotel together still deep in conversation. Filippo spent a few more days in Rome at the Piazza Farnase home he rented from the German press attaché Molier. He saw his friend and landlord, as well as a few older acquaintances, including Enzo Ferrari, but the intense heat and the uncertainty about the future made it difficult to relax. On September 1 Filippo didn't dare to leave the house, fearing what could happen during an anticipated Fascist uprising.

The day after that, he went to the passport office to collect Anja's documents, but they were not yet ready. The embassy refused to issue the visa before seeing a medical certificate proving that she needed treatment. It was not the best time to be reliant on a clunking bureaucracy. Every day that Anja remained in Rome was potentially a day closer to her doom, even if she didn't see it like that.

Filippo was at least satisfied that his wife was well provided for financially. She received a 12,000 lire monthly allowance from him, and had 50,000 lire in savings and other securities valued at 36,000. If she needed to free up more cash, she had an ample collection of expensive fur coats and jewellery, worth some 70,000 lire. She could also call on Giacomo for help, if necessary. Filippo left Rome on September 2 with a lawyer friend, who was going on to Brindisi via Cerignola. The Allies landed their first troops on the Italian mainland at Bagnara in Calabria on September 3. More troops arrived at Salerno and Taranto over the coming days.

To begin with, the Baron busied himself with work on his estates and was reassured after receiving a telegram from Anja, telling him that she was safe. He was rankled when the town mayor of Puglia ordered him to host a dinner for German army officers stationed in the province. Manfredi later described it as a "Fascist order" and insisted he had no choice in the matter, just as he could not refuse when, back in August, a young German officer had for a time been billeted on the Cerignola estate.

Fearing that the estate might itself be bombed, Manfredi sent all his staff away and went to stay with friends. He received a second telegram from Anja saying that her papers were in order and she was ready to leave. Manfredi telegrammed Koehler and asked him to make travel arrangements. He heard nothing back and on September 7, the day before the new Italian government signed an Armistice with the Allies, Anja sent another telegram to her husband to say she was now staying in the Grand Hotel and still awaiting transport. It was the last message he received from her and, as we shall see, it was a lie. The next day, the Baron found both wireless and telephone communications were out and there was no way to contact Rome.

On September 9, Allied forces arrived in Salerno and Taranto, with the Fifth and Eighth Armies advancing up the country to create a line from Salerno in the West coast to Bari on the East. The Prime Minister, Field Marshall Badoglio, and the King, fled Rome to set up a new government in South Italy, allowing the Nazis to forcibly occupy most of northern and central Italy, eventually rescuing Mussolini on September 12. The old fascist headed up a puppet government headquartered in Salo and designed to lend an air of credibility to Nazi rule.

Before the Allied invasion, the Germans had just three divisions on the Italian mainland, with another four on Sicily. Three months later, the Nazis had shifted nineteen divisions to the country, eight more than the Allies. While by that point the Allies had taken Naples, the Germans had managed to get a numerical advantage and were well dug in to defend Rome for months. Thanks to the initial inertia by the Badoglio government and confusion among Italian forces as to whether or not they should round on their former German allies, British and American forces were unable to advance up the country as swiftly as they otherwise might. Fierce fighting would continue for nearly another year. Hitler assigned one of his favourite generals, Field Marshall Albert Kesselring, to command all the German forces in Italy (Rommel had initially taken command of the forces in the north, but was later recalled to Germany, after being implicated in the July 20, 1944, plot to assassinate Hitler).

The sudden occupation meant a huge shift in life for Italians living in the German zone. The Baron was no longer at liberty to move around as he pleased. He was stopped in his car at a German road block the day after it began, but unlike many other forms of transport, the car was not requisitioned because it was gas powered. He took the opportunity to hide it on the Rio Morte estate. The Germans did however confiscate his motorcycle. The physical occupation of Cerignola didn't last long, and most German troops soon withdrew, although an 8pm curfew remained. Manfredi later described his actions throughout this bewildering period:

> During those days I continued to travel by bicycle all over the district to give encouragement to my people who were terrified at what had happened, robberies, pillage, and acts of violence of every description. I also wanted to hear from the Italian soldiers, who were returning home, all about the probable location of German troops.

Such dark days for Cerignola did not last long, because the region was liberated within weeks and its Italian Royal Air Force base transformed into an important staging ground for the Allies. But before that happened, not wanting to become a pawn of the Nazi occupiers, Baron Manfredi made the decision to break through the Allied lines to Bari. His wife might have gotten along famously with Himmler, but the Baron wanted to help Britain and America rid his country of the Germans. It was a mistake he would regret for the rest of his life.

---

[26] Manfredi files.
[27] See Schellenberg (book), p.302.
[28] Zimmer files.
[29] Rauff files.
[30] Waller, p.160.
[31] Schellenberg files, National Archives.
[32] See Schellenberg (book), p.329.
[33] See Schellenberg (book), p.295.
[34] See Wulff, Wilhelm.

Manfredi Captured

Baron Manfredi shivered as he stepped from the plane and onto the runway at Prestwick airport. It was January 8, 1944, and the chilly weather on Scotland's west coast, looking across the Firth of Clyde to the Isle of Arran, was a far cry from the sunny climes of Cerignola, let alone Algiers, where the Baron had been sequestered by Britain's Secret Intelligence Service (SIS), otherwise known as MI6, for the past week. Manfredi's landing card listed him under the alias of Gianni Bianchi, a cover name chosen for him by his captors. Under the heading "purpose of journey" the words "required in London" had been typed. Certainly, the Baron had been given no say in the matter. Manfredi had holidayed only once in England, back in 1926. Now, he feared, he might never be going home to Italy.

Allied intelligence agencies struggled to determine the ultimate loyalty of Italians, generally, and particularly during the period of civil war that erupted in the wake of the Allied invasion. To summarise; Italy entered the war as an Axis power on June 10, 1940. Three years later, on July 10, 1943, Allied troops invaded Sicily. Italy capitulated and signed the Armistice on September 3, the day when British forces arrived on the mainland at Reggio Calabria. More Allied troops landed on September 9 at Salerno and Taranto. Meanwhile, in the north of the country, Germany bolstered its forces, effectively dividing the country in two. After springing Mussolini from prison, the Nazi-controlled north was ostensibly ruled by his Salo Government. Partisan organisations immediately sprang up to oppose both the regime and the German occupation. Meanwhile, the south declared war on Germany on October 13, while just under 100,000 Italian troops agreed to keep fighting for the Axis powers. Elsewhere, such as on the Greek island of Cephallonia, captured Italian forces were summarily executed by the Germans. In total, by September 14, Germany had either completely or partially disarmed some eighty five Italian divisions and captured 700,000 soldiers. As the Western Allies advanced up the country, how could they be sure who was friend and who was foe?

Winston Churchill had long identified Italy as the "soft underbelly" of the Axis powers, and saw her defeat as the surest way to crush Hitler. Fulfilling this vision was more challenging than he had hoped, but it would have been even more difficult if the Germans had been able to create an effective stay-behind network of saboteurs and guerilla fighters, wreaking havoc behind enemy lines. Hitler's Italian spies had to be rooted out. Yet the Allied forces knew this would be an uphill battle.

As early as March 1940, MI6 had complained about the difficulties in recruiting Italian spies. Attempts were made to find agents in Sicily and Libya (then under Italian control) as well as some half-cocked efforts in New York, Argentina, Brazil and Canada. Captain FW Winterbotham, MI6's Air Service liaison officer, called the situation "lamentable". "I cannot believe," he wrote in one memo, "that Italian Air Force Officers in Budapest, Italian engineers and merchants in Belgrade and Sofia are all unapproachable. This is the side from which we need to penetrate since the French use their own opportunities to the utmost."[35]

The Allied advance into Libya in February 1941 provided further opportunities to develop Italian agents who could be re-inserted back into their home territory, after Australian forces captured some 100,000 prisoners. But the head of the Middle East Section, Captain Cuthbert Bowlby, warned, "Italians make very bad agents and although many of them dislike the Fascist regime, yet they love their country and dislike danger. I am afraid that any attempt of this kind will merely be treated as a beneficial repatriation scheme."[36]

Other efforts included trying to recruit a musician due to play at a festival in Venice in September 1942 (he was asked to observe which battleships were in Venice) and the creation of a fake film company in Portugal that could visit Italy under the ruse of looking for locations. There is no record of these ideas bearing fruit. A further plan was to recruit Italians being repatriated from East Africa, but it was noted that this had already been tried and the "Fascist special police [the OVRA]" had taken "very active steps" to stop people speaking to potential British agents. On one occasion, it was feared that "the worst may have happened to the one useful contact that was made".

By the time of the Allied landings, Italy was a virtual intelligence blackspot. An MI6 unit had been embedded with the 15th Army Group, under the cover of the No 1 Intelligence Unit, and with the invasion it became the SIS vanguard in Italy.[37] Yet even with boots on the ground, the army group's leader, General Sir Harold Alexander, cabled to London on August 29 that, "Up to present in Sicily, SIS unit has not been able to provide any reports of tactical importance and in my opinion it is not likely that they will be able to do so in future except in the case of prolonged static conditions." Things began to improve in October 1943, when the MI6 unit was taken over by John Bruce Lockhart, a former schoolmaster and rising star in the service. Under his command, security, recruitment and training were all tightened up and the unit's HQ was established in Bari (codenamed 44200), where operations could be directed both into the German-occupied north, and the Balkans and central Europe.

One subsection of the group developed close ties with the Italian Military Intelligence Service (SIM), which had essential access to sources in the army and in right-wing circles. Lockhart also set about helping to establish Italian opposition groups, including by giving backing to the Communists.

The task of penetrating northern Italy was handed to Major Brian Ashford-Russell, a left-handed ex-Commando who had lost the use of his dominant hand and been taken prisoner in North Africa. He had an unusual knack for successfully recruiting Italians and was praised by Lockhart as "very loyal" and commended for running his section "like clockwork". By the end of the war, Lockhart later recalled, MI6 had up to forty undercover wireless operators sending back information daily about German troop movements and order of battle.

Sadly, at least one of Ashford-Russell's agents met with an untimely end. Code-named Dragonfly, he had been recruited in South America and spent four months in Rome where he sent back voluminous reports via wireless. Dragonfly enjoyed regular lunches with the SS chief in Rome, Herbert Kappler, and — even though he sensed he was in danger — argued that "risks had sometimes to be taken". Dragonfly managed to burn his papers as SS troops stormed his residence, but he was later shot at Dachau.

But most central to the mission being undertaken in Italy was the work of British codebreakers back home at Bletchley Park, who were busy deciphering intercepted German communications. It was chiefly through them that men like Lockhart and Ashford-Russell determined who they could, or could not, trust. They learnt, for example, that the Nazis had been building a stay-behind network of Fascist terrorists and informers who were being primed to puncture the occupation from within. There were more than fifty names on the list. The Baron's was amongst them.

Baron Filippo Manfredi had many friends in the world of espionage, naturally in the SIM, rather than the Italian equivalent of the Gestapo, the OVRA. Towards the end of September 1943, he was visited in Fascist-held Cerignola by two SIM operatives, who arrived at his estate on bicycles after deserting from Rome. They intended to cross Allied lines and deliver information about German and Italian troops, firing capacity, and stocks of petrol and ammunition, as well as to offer a proposal for the Allies to make a landing south of Rome. The pair also carried with them a plan to form a new Liberal Party and the draft of a constitution for a new monarchist government.

One of the men was an old friend of Manfredi's — the legendary Errol Flynn lookalike Prince Raimondo Lanza di Trabia. Lanza was by now an adjutant to the head of the SIM, General Carboni, who was hiding in Rome. Lanza wanted to tell the Allies where he was. The trio spent the night at a friend's home, drinking wine, reminiscing, and planning their route for the following day. The Baron decided to go over to the Allies. After all, both his wife and stepson were now stranded in German territory in the north. He needed the invading army to win the war if his family was to survive it.

The spies gave Manfredi fake papers in the name of a Sergeant Renato Lima. His cover story was that he was on leave to visit his family. The trio set off on the road to Andria, but soon adopted the backroads out of fear of being stopped at a German roadblock. Another of Manfredi's aristocratic friends, Count Spagnoletti, put them up for the night. He also passed them information about safer routes into Bari, where they would be free from German interference. The men were able to cross into Allied territory unmolested on the night of September 22. But the Baron was cycling blithely into a nest of spies.

In Bari, Prince Lanza and the other SIM man left Manfredi and went on to Brindisi. Manfredi went to find Colonel Geronazzo, the head of the carabinieri in the city and yet another old friend. Geronazzo had previously told the Baron that if the situation should deteriorate in Italy, he should try to contact him. In return, Geronazzo had sent an officer on a fact-finding mission through Foggia, and part of his mission was to contact Manfredi. The pair had missed each other when Manfredi left with Prince Lanza. Manfredi explained everything he knew about German troop positions. As far as Manfredi was concerned, he had done his part for Italy and by extension the Allied cause.

Manfredi remained in Bari for several days, but by the end of the month the Allies had advanced through Foggia and up to Cerignola, so it was safe for him to return to his estates, where he threw himself back into oil and wine production. At the same time, he handed over the Palazzo Manfredi to the Allies to use as a base — another good turn for the side he wanted to win the war. During October, Manfredi visited Bari twice more, both times for leisure, confidant that the conflict in Italy was going in the right direction. But he was blissfully unaware that he was being regarded with suspicion and under observation by Bruce Lockhart's MI6 agents.

SIS had learnt through "most secret sources" — the secret name for information deciphered by Britain's Enigma codebreakers — that Manfredi had been in contact with German intelligence and was earmarked to form part of the stay-behind network. The loose commitment Filippo had made to Koehler in exchange for help with Anja's passage to Switzerland had most probably been forgotten by the Italian. After all, Cerignola had been liberated and it didn't seem likely that Koehler would be calling in the favour any time soon. In any case, the German had not held up his end of the bargain by helping to get Anja out of the country. But Koehler had evidently reported Manfredi's 'recruitment' to his superiors and the message had been intercepted by the British.

As far as MI6 was concerned, there was no immediate need to bring the Baron in for questioning, but pressure from the Eighth Army forced their hand. Further information had been received from an Italian intelligence liaison officer, who told how Manfredi had been suspected of working for German intelligence for two years. The Baron had apparently been placed under observation by the SIM, but never suspected a thing. We don't know the name of the officer involved, but one likely candidate is Manfredi's supposed friend, Gianni Hecht, who had only recently returned from visiting Anja in Switzerland.

Still blissfully unaware of the impending catastrophe hanging over him, Manfredi travelled to Bari again on October 29, 1943, with 1,000 lire in his pocket and a suitcase packed for what was supposed to be a weekend break. He checked in, as he often did, at the Hotel Imperial. The Baron had barely begun to unpack when there was a firm knock at the apartment door. His arrest and subsequent interrogation was no doubt undertaken with the utmost politeness, but Manfredi would have been under no illusion about the seriousness of the accusations.

Manfredi was sequestered in a flat in Bari for two weeks with a Major Del Curto and interrogated by at least one MI6 officer and another man from the Combined Services Detailed Interrogation Centre (CSDIC), probably a British Army officer or an officer from MI9. At the same time, agents detained and questioned several other people Manfredi had spoken with during the previous forty eight hours, including workers on his estate, although no evidence was found against him as a result. In fact, the initial finding was that rather than being pro-German, Manfredi had done his best to keep his nose out of Fascist affairs. A subsequent note sent to the MI5 spymaster Helenus 'Buster' Milmo concluded that the report from the unnamed Italian intelligence officer had been "ill-founded". Indeed, the mission Manfredi had undertaken with Prince Lanza was evidence of his antipathy towards the Germans. And there was something else — Manfredi was holding up poorly in the Bari flat. "His nerves, already strained by the long delay in reaching a final decision, have given way badly and he has been drinking heavily and taking quantities of caffeine," the agent reported back.

To explain Manfredi's absence from his estates, it was circulated in Bari and Cerignola that he was being questioned about the activities of his suspect wife, a not-unreasonable cover story that would do little harm to his reputation if he was later found to be innocent. Meanwhile, one MI6 officer told Manfredi that they were holding onto him because they wanted to use his knowledge of Rome and its society when the city was taken. This might have gone some way to mitigate his fury at the injustice of being held against his will.

During this time, Manfredi's captors failed to extract any useful information. As a last resort, they brought in the Baron's mistress, Senora D'Amati, to speak to him 'in private'. She implored her lover to come clean, while he loudly wracked his brains for "any reason why he should have been unjustly accused of espionage". An MI6 officer "listened dutifully at the keyhole" but nothing of any use was gleaned.

The interrogator concluded that it was "psychologically impossible for the man to have been a German agent; that he is neither Fascist nor pro-

German; that he was an impulsive and confiding child, for example his servants held the key to his safe; he was temperamentally incapable of keeping any important secret." That last point wasn't strictly true — Manfredi said nothing of Anja's meeting with Himmler in the Spring, although he would later insist that he had.

After two weeks, no real evidence had been unearthed, giving the Allies a major headache. The information in the Manfredi case had not been obtained via some unreliable captured agent whose evidence could be discounted. Instead, it had come from German intercepts decoded at Bletchley Park under Alan Turing and colleagues, including star mathematician Herbert Hart. Koehler had told his bosses that Manfredi had been recruited as a stay-behind agent. The word 'saboteur' had no doubt been included. Such intercepts were almost always referred to as "Most Secret Sources". But as the report accompanying Manfredi to England spelt out in plain language:

> Undoubtedly Manfredi has put up a very plausible defence and we cannot entirely write off the possibility that the SD were simply indulging in window dressing in claiming him as their agent. However, in view of the very damning evidence against both him and his wife provided by Hart's sources, we clearly cannot be unduly influenced by the conclusions of an able but inexperienced interrogator working under difficult conditions.

The issue at stake was a grave one. If the information in the decrypted cable was wrong — by design or otherwise — then what else was awry? Could the Germans be playing a game of misdirection, forcing the Allies to round up dozens of innocent men while the real saboteurs went undetected? And what wider implications would that have? Could it be that the Germans knew their code had been broken?

A further note sent back to MI6 HQ on December 14, 1943, made clear that Manfredi should be questioned by more seasoned interrogators:

> Nevertheless we still think it desirable that Manfredi should be brought to the UK for further interrogation. Not only are there several points which have not

yet been adequately cleared up, but we think that on principle this case should be investigated as thoroughly as possible. Manfredi is the first alleged agent of the SD in Italy to fall into our hands; we regard him as providing us with a test case of the reality or the reverse of the SD's post occupational network. As you are aware we have not far short of fifty names of non-Germans in Italy alleged to be involved in the SD. As we advance up Italy we may reasonably expect that the question how far we can rely on evidence from our most secret material unsupported from any outside source will become increasingly urgent. If only the question of Manfredi's guilt or innocence can be finally settled, it will be of great assistance to us in dealing with similar cases.

Almost two months after deciding to take a short holiday, Filippo was finally freed from the flat in Bari only to be whisked some 500km away to a safe house in Algiers, while the British took care of some legal niceties. The "quite specific" information from MSS, coupled with the report from the Italian intelligence officer, concerned the British, particularly Herbert Hart at Bletchley Park, who wrote in a memo that "we are certainly agreeable" to Manfredi being transferred to Britain for more intensive interrogation.

Buster Milmo took care of the paperwork with the immigration department, which had to legally sign off such operations. He noted that his spies were still skeptical of the Italian's guilt. One had recently written that: "At the time of his removal to Algiers he was in a highly excited state, and I feel it is possible that a period of further interrogation and confinement might result in a complete nervous collapse." The author of the note believed this had nothing to do with Manfredi's guilt, but rather that he was worried about his estates and the end of his relationship with his mistress. Another cause of Manfredi's anxiety was the "natural instability of his character".

Milmo's fellow officer Kim Philby, himself an as-yet-undiscovered Soviet double agent, also raised a concern. He noted that Manfredi's detention might lead to "awkward questions" from the Italians, given that there was no evidence against him that they could produce. However, he was, in the end, supportive of the extradition, adding that the British "need not, of course, show much concern for Italian feelings, but it is thought that in view of the source of our information he might be better out of the way".

It was now January 1944, and nearly two decades after his one and only trip to the United Kingdom, Baron Filippo Manfredi de Blasiis was on his way back, against his will, furious and bewildered. He could only think to blame two people: his slippery German contact Gerhard Koehler, and his troublesome wife Anja who, as far as he knew, might not even be alive.

---

[35] Jeffery, p.423-427.
[36] Ibid.
[37] Ibid, p.476-500.

ILLUSTRATIONS

Anja and Judith Bergroth in their younger days

Top: Oskar Bergroth. Below: Sigrid Winter

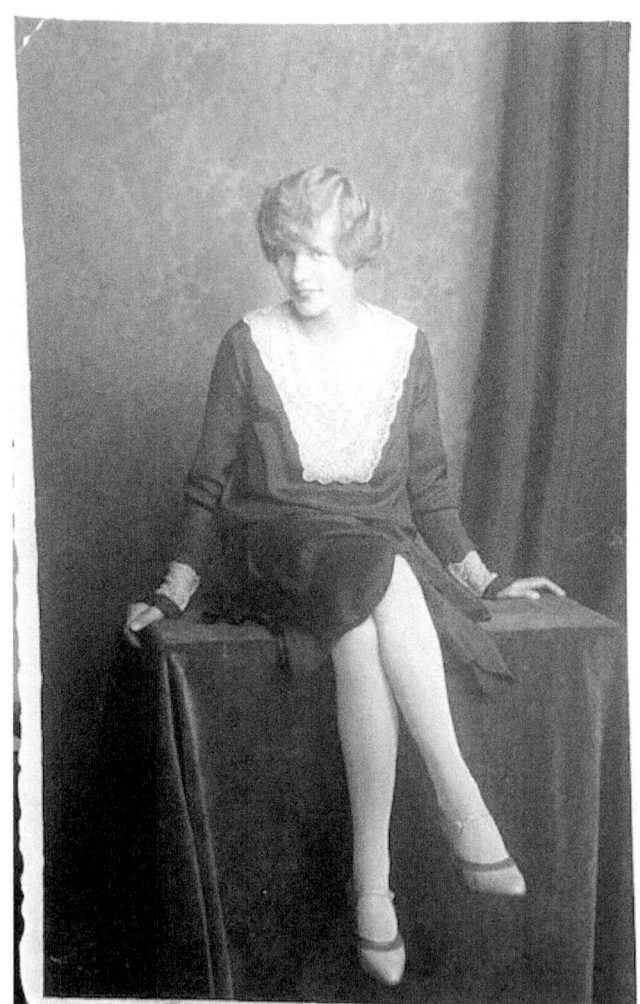

Anja in Hamburg in 1929

Gunned down by his prospective father-in-law: Gunnar Aspelin

Husband number one: Anja and Hans Götz

Mother and son: Anja and Aldo Götz

Captured: Baron Manfredi in MI5 mugshot

Baron Manfredi in happier times

Baron Manfredi's interrogator Robin 'Tin Eye' Stephens of MI5

Himmler with Margarete and Gudrun

The odd couple: Margarete and Himmler

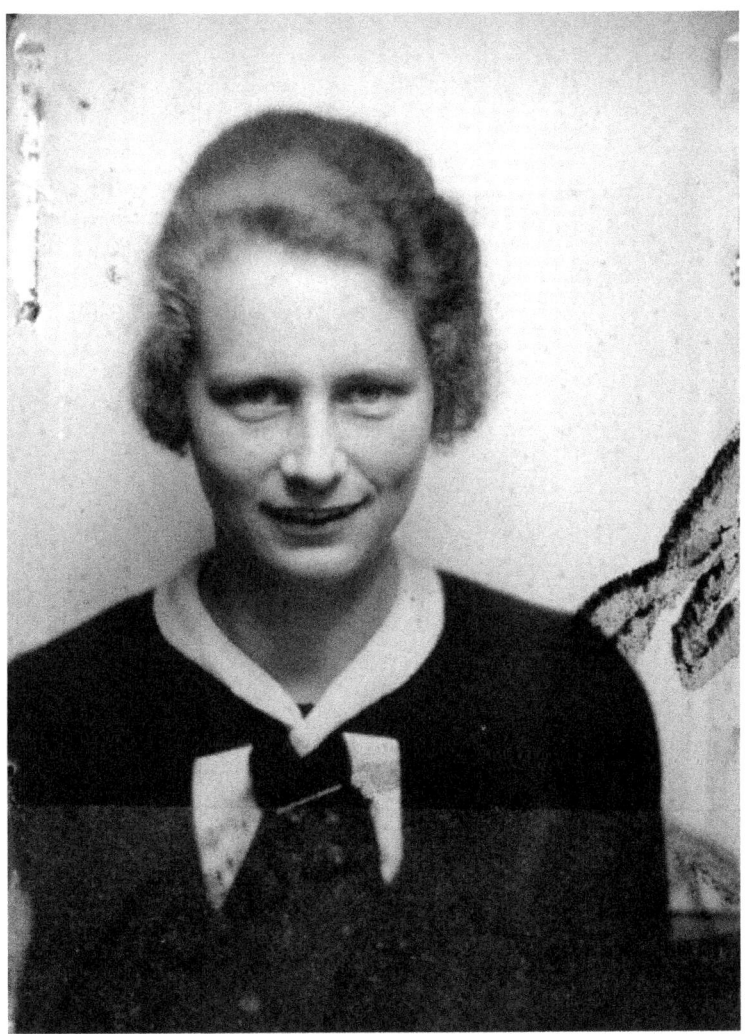

Himmler's sporty 'second wife' Hedwig Potthast

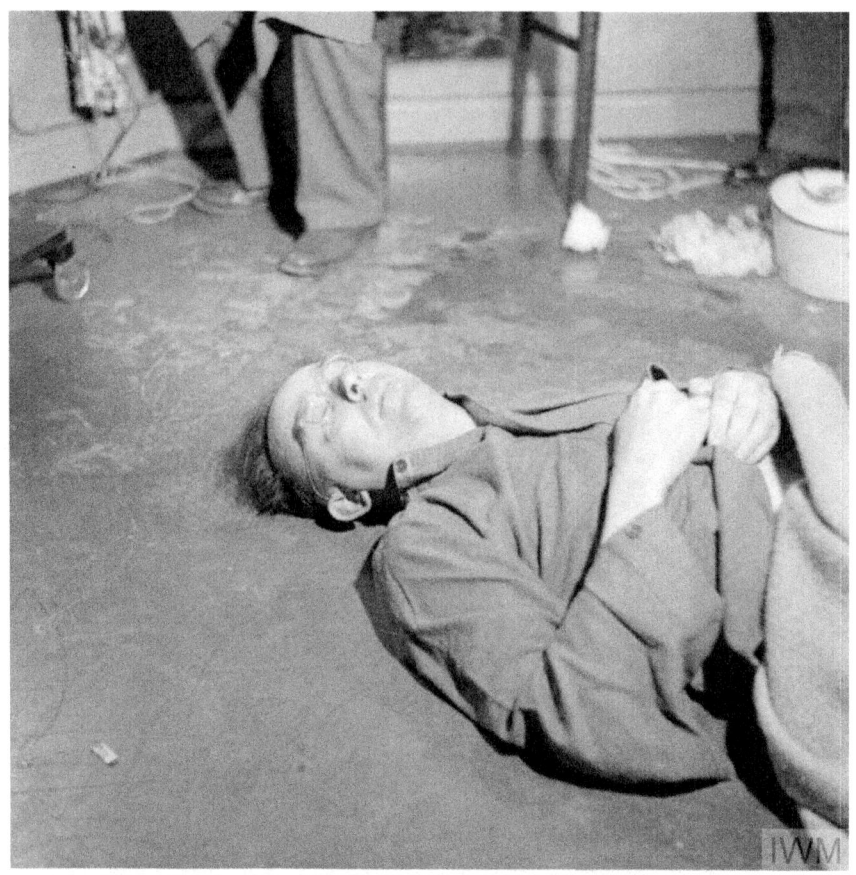

Himmler dead in Allied custody after biting cyanide capsule

Anja's 'uncle', the Finnish diplomat Onni Talas

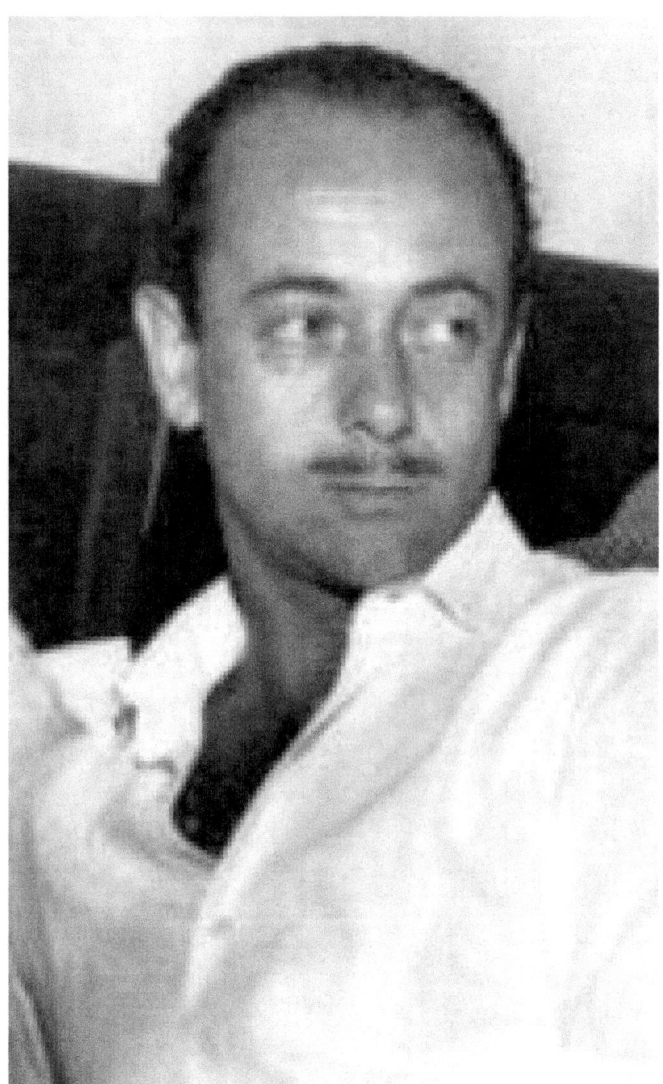

Baron Manfredi's dear friend Prince Raimondo Lanza di Trabia, who encouraged him to cross Allied lines into Bari

Anja's beloved doctor Janos Plesch

Allen Dulles, future CIA chief who brokered the Nazi surrender in Italy

Anja's handler Klaus Hügel, who risked Himmler's wrath by calling for her to be removed from Italy

Guido Zimmer's star agent Andreas Zolyomy

Himmler's scheming therapist Felix Kersten

Partisan leader Ferrucio Parri, who Anja planned to seduce

Count Folke Bernadotte held talks with Himmler and Schellenberg

Fanatical Nazi and RSHA chief Ernst Kaltenbrunner

The knowingly handsome Karl Wolff

Psychopathic Gestapo prison boss Theodor Saeveke

Himmler's trusted foreign spy chief Walter Schellenberg

Himmler's astrologer Wilhelm Wulff

Manfredi Confesses

ost enemy agents arrived at Camp 020 with nothing more than their uniform, a few personal letters and their service revolver. But Baron Manfredi was a unique case. His belongings when he checked in on January 10, 1944, read more like a list of items one might pack for a holiday which, of course, he had. Among them was a wrist watch with a metal strap, a gold cigarette lighter, several flannel shirts, loose collars, socks, cuffs and pyjamas, as well as three bottles of medication and a riding crop. There was one, single, odd sock. The Baron was also carrying a photograph of his wife Anja and his adopted son Aldo.

Based in a sprawling Victorian-built mansion named Latchmere House in Richmond, South West London, Camp 020 was Britain's interrogation centre for captured German spies. Overseen by MI5's colourful and controversial Lieutenant-Colonel Robin Stephens, nicknamed Tin Eye on account of the monocle he habitually wore over his right eye, it had been integral in recruiting some eleven agents for Britain's Double Cross programme, including the celebrated turncoats

TATE, ZIG-ZAG, and MUTT and JEFF. But the first stage of any successful recruitment was to break the detainee and make him confess, in excruciating detail if possible. That was where Tin Eye came in.

Stephens was beloved by his staff and was known to be kind, generous and loyal, but he was also an iron-hard spybreaker, who peppered his written reports on captured agents with florid and often xenophobic turns of phrase. For example, Stephens had the following view on Italians: "Italy is a country peopled by undersized, posturing folk."[38] Tin Eye nicknamed these reports, printed on bright yellow paper to make them stand out amid other documents, Yellow Perils.

Typically, a suspect arriving at Camp 020 would be stripped and subjected to a full body search. After one prisoner was found to be concealing writing materials in a false tooth, this included a dental examination. All inmates were issued with basic flannel trousers and a coat, with a six-inch diamond shape sewn in to indicate their status as an enemy spy. The induction process would be undertaken in almost complete silence, with guards ordered not to talk to the prisoner or answer any questions, before placing them in a cell alone. Later, their personal details would be recorded and a photograph taken, while a doctor would give them a thorough examination. Very soon afterwards, the prisoner would be marched into the interrogation room, usually to face the penetrating glare of Tin Eye Stephens and a panel of officers.

The inmate would be made to stand throughout a barrage of questions, and would usually not be given time to respond. There was to be no friendliness or comfort for the suspects. Stephens argued there should be, "No chivalry. No gossip. No cigarettes...Figuratively, a spy in war should be at the point of a bayonet." Stephens later used the analogy that the interrogation should be treated like a court of law, where the defendant stands to answer questions before a judge. It was, he argued, "a question of atmosphere".

After the war, Stephens faced a court martial for alleged mistreatment of prisoners at the Bad Nenndorf camp in Germany, although he was cleared of all charges. The fact that Tin Eye escaped conviction for mistreating prisoners is no surprise — he always strongly insisted that there was to be no violence towards Camp 020 inmates. "Violence is taboo," he said, "for not only does it produce answers to please, but it lowers the standard of information."

However, the absence of physical violence did not mean that all the tactics used at the camp were pleasant. There was the constant threat of execution, both real and implied. Britain executed sixteen spies during the war and fourteen of them had been broken at Camp 020. Stephens felt even more should have faced the ultimate punishment. Most of the cells were bugged, while Stephens also made extensive use of stool pigeons, who would cozy up to inmates and then later betray their confidence. Another psychological trick was the threatened use of Cell Fourteen, a padded room left unchanged from Latchmere House's days as a psychiatric institution. Prisoners would sometimes break after being told they would be locked inside Cell Fourteen, with its ominous overtones, although in reality nothing happened there and, besides the walls, it was the same as any other cell. Drugs and alcohol were also used to loosen up inmates, but such experimental techniques were usually deemed unreliable.

Despite the tough regime, the camp was not a living hell. Those who did not agree to become double agents, or who were otherwise thought too dangerous to release before the end of the war, had access to recreation rooms, gardens, a library, and were able to cook their own food, with similar rations to British soldiers. The camp was not a PoW facility, so was outside the Geneva Conventions, and it was not listed by the Red Cross. However, only three people ever tried to escape, all unsuccessfully, and only one of three suicide attempts succeeded. But it's safe to say that Baron Manfredi did not enjoy his time in South West London.

Although a fairly handsome man, with an appearance not dissimilar to a middle-aged Robert De Niro, the casual reader would not have guessed it from elements of his Yellow Peril report that read: "Complexion: ruddy, sallow. Head: Large. Nose: On large side. Mouth: Big, thick lips." Manfredi was 5'9" and "well built", and the otherwise unflattering description did at least conclude with the more charitable line: "No peculiarities." Under the heading for hobbies, interests and sports, was the entry: "All sports". While under "vices and weaknesses" the spies had written: "Smokes. Has mistress." Signora D'Amati was now a long way away, of course. It was also noted that Manfredi was a registered Fascist, but that he insisted he held no true allegiance to the party.

The summary of Manfredi's case, written in the unmistakably brash style of Tin Eye Stephens, highlighted how unlucky the Italian had been. He had never been considered a dangerous enemy. Instead, his detention was only about proving or otherwise the integrity of Most Secret Sources and the apparent naivety of his original interrogators in Bari:

> The case of Baron Manfredi is the disastrous story of an Intelligence Officer in Italy who, having failed to extract a confession from a spy on perfectly good evidence, went right out of his way to champion his innocence. He was backed by his Intelligence organisation in Italy. In the result, the authenticity of Source inevitably came into question and the evidence against some fifty other suspected persons was held doubtful. SIS accordingly determined to have Manfredi flown to this country, not so much to prove the case against Manfredi himself, but to re-establish once and for all the incontestable nature of their Source.

The fact that Manfredi had been cleared by his captors in Bari was known to him, and this annoyed Stephens greatly. Knowing he had already been judged innocent by his interrogators made Manfredi "highly indignant and recalcitrant". "Fortified with this knowledge, Manfredi practiced the tantrums of his race and hardly a word of sense could be extracted from him," he added.

Stephens decided to enlist the help of another Italian captive, the "self-styled co-belligerent" Captain Andres Angel Bonzo, who was brought in to aid translation during interrogation and then report back on whatever Manfredi told him privately in their cell. This stool pigeon was a Vatican lawyer and secret agent of the SIM, who Stephens believed was the "best of the Italians" in the camp, on account of the fact that, in Stephens' view, he had always worked in the interests of Italy, rather than Mussolini. The fact that Bonzo was willing to rat out his fellow countrymen to curry favour with the British was another advantage.

It was a sneaky tactic used frequently at the camp. Bonzo was brought in to help translate, and the pair were allowed to retire to a cell together after the interrogation. In this way, Bonzo was able to continue the questioning surreptitiously while MI5 officers secretly listened in.

Manfredi maintained his complete innocence until the night of January 22, 1944. Finally, he admitted making a promise to Koehler that he would help the Germans, but insisted that it had simply been a bluff to obtain a favour in return. Stephens was not satisfied with this answer. Even though he had never heard of Koehler, Stephens "decided to bluff". He insisted that Koehler was a well-known German intelligence operative, and therefore Manfredi had just admitted the central charge against him — that he was a Nazi stay behind agent, albeit one who had not yet actually committed any acts of espionage. Stephens told him he wanted more information:

> Many were the gesticulations that accompanied his prompt denials, and confusion became worse confounded when Bonzo joined in the fray. They were both dismissed to the same cell. Pressure has since been maintained, either by interrogation or by the persistent arguments which have resulted between Manfredi and Bonzo.

Over the course of the next day, Manfredi handed in two further statements that fleshed out his case, writing:

> When I replied that I was ready to do anything to help my country, Koehler said that he would send someone down to me in Puglia to commit acts of sabotage according to plans which would be agreed later between us. I accepted the general idea in order to gain time and Koehler told me that I was not to tell the Italian General staff about the matter, nor would he inform anyone. The following day I immediately told Colonel de Carlo about the proposition made to me and he told me to let the matter drop.

In the second statement, Manfredi insisted that he told Koehler he was only willing to help Italy, not the Germans per se. Stephens was informed of the contents of the statements the next morning and triumphantly confronted Manfredi. However, thanks to an "imperfect brief" Stephens got the wrong end of the stick, believing Manfredi had confessed to planning to blow up bridges on his own estate. A "monstrous argument" took place between the pair and the accusation was "met by Manfredi with frenzied eyes, wild ejaculations and intricate gesticulation". As Manfredi quite sensibly pointed out, "In my estate there is no water, there is no need of bridges. Where there are no bridges, they cannot be blown up. For that I am manacled and brought from my country to England."

Still, once the dust had settled, the admissions satisfied Stephens immensely. He wrote:

> The primary object of the investigation, namely, to re-establish once and for all the incontestable nature of SIS Source, was thus achieved.... The secondary object of the investigation, that is to say the espionage case against Manfredi, was also attained.

Stephens argued that the character of Manfredi as assessed by the MI6 team in Italy was "nonsense". "Far from being a 'confiding child', he kept dangerous information to himself," the report said. Stephens added:

> [Manfredi] completely deceived the Intelligence authorities in Italy and he put up a tolerable fight at Camp 020. Always providing the Germans were on the winning side, he would have worked faithfully for them. He talked merely because he was caught. Then, characteristic of his treacherous race, he posed, and for a time was accepted, as a friend to England. In my opinion, his breeding and his education aggravate his espionage offence. His subsequent lack of scruple places Manfredi beyond the pale. I have no sympathy for Manfredi and I hope none will be had for him at the end of the war.

It was a harsh judgment, considering that Manfredi had done very little to aid the Nazis. In fact, it could be argued that the Baron had done far more to help the Allies than he had the Germans, considering the dangerous mission across Allied lines that he had undertaken with Prince Lanza.

Stephens also had something to say about Anja and her husband's understanding of her meeting with Himmler. Stephens had "strong grounds for the belief that Baroness Manfredi is an agent of the German Secret Service under high patronage". To this end, Manfredi had been questioned extensively, and relayed the story of her meeting with Himmler and what Stephens said was her "supposed" medical treatment in Zurich. Clearly, Tin Eye had his doubts about the extent of Anja's illness. However, Manfredi was unable to supply much information, partly because he had seen his wife only a couple of times since the meeting with Himmler, and had received no communications from her since September 1943. Still, Stephens believed Manfredi knew more than he was letting on:

> Manfredi would have us believe that the choice of Berchtesgaden was fortuitous and that the actions of Himmler were merely those of a chivalrous gentleman. It is significant, however, on her return to Rome, that the woman boasted of her meeting with Himmler. Indeed, so notorious did she become that Colonel di Carlo reprimanded her for her indiscretion. The odds were, of course, that Baroness Manfredi, like her husband, was a spy, and it is now satisfactory to record confirmation has been received to the effect that she is in fact a paid agent of the German Secret Service. A postscript to this case is that Manfredi resolutely maintains he divulged to the Intelligence authorities at Bari the fact that his wife had met Himmler at Berchtesgaden. This information does not appear in any reports.

Manfredi was given some benefit of the doubt where his wife was concerned; Stephens recognised their strained relationship meant he was unlikely to know everything she had been up to. "In spite of the fact that Manfredi is loath to admit that he had little in common with the Baroness, this may be the explanation for his not knowing of his wife's secret activities," Stephens wrote.

A few days after the 'confession' that Manfredi had been "recruited by the Germans", Buster Milmo wrote to a Home Office official to tell him the news. "[Manfredi] is, however, still withholding a great deal of information and is definitely lying on many points". Milmo suggested holding onto the Baron at least until the end of the war. It was not until October 1944 that formal instructions for Manfredi's internment were received, with permission for three other inmates coming at the same time — Marcello Mochi, Otto Mayer and Hans Scharf.

Baron Manfredi was finally flown back to Italy on June 1, 1945, after spending almost two years in custody. The Roman Catholic chivalric society to which he belonged, the Order of Malta, or Knights of Malta, had begun asking questions about Manfredi's whereabouts, prompting his release. Manfredi had some company on the plane, fellow prisoners Marcello Mochi, Ferrucio Furlani and Alfredo Manna all departed Blackbushe Airport together.

As Stephens later wrote in the official history of Camp 020:

> There was more of Poncinello in Manfredi than of Machiavelli, but even Bonzo, who co-belligerated the Baron in a bread raid on the prison pantry, found his company more nauseating in the ultimate than it was amusing. They left [Camp 020] on different dates to go their separate ways: Bonzo to work for the Italian General Staff, Manfredi to face its music.

In fact, the Baron faced no further punishment on his return to Italy.

Meanwhile, a new inmate was still settling into life at Camp 020. SS-Sturmbannführer Dr Klaus Hügel had arrived in May 1945, ready to give his interrogators as much information as they required. As it turned out, Hügel knew much more about Anja Manfredi de Blasiis than her husband did. Because while Manfredi had been in captivity — being drilled at Camp 020 for information he didn't have — his wife was back in Italy, holding talks with him about an espionage mission that could well have changed the course of the war.

---

38 See Hoare for more on Stephens and Camp 020.

Feminine Charm

Sturmbannführer Dr Klaus Hügel was captured on April 28, 1945, in Como, not far from the Swiss border, as the Western Allies advanced up the countryside in the wake of the Nazi's capitulation in Italy. Whether or not he was at the time attempting to flee is impossible to know, but his captors had this to say of him: "Source is pleasant and intelligent and fully cooperative. He expressed anti-Nazi sentiments which are not thought to be entirely insincere. However, a sense of guilt and fear of the consequences of his long association with the SS and SD, have undoubtedly helped to bring about his present attitude." Hügel was subsequently able to give a very detailed account of the procedures of the Nazi's foreign intelligence service, the Ausland-SD, otherwise known as Amt VI of the RSHA, from methods of recruitment and training, to the steps taken to create post-occupational networks in Italy and other territories. The Allies thought Hügel to be highly reliable.

In his mid-thirties, Hügel had brown hair, grey eyes, a round face, a fresh complexion and a scar across his forehead.[39] The son of a Freiburg lawyer, Hügel had followed in his father's footsteps and graduated with his own law degree in 1937. But rather than enter into private practice he joined the civil service as an assessor at the district office in Konstanz and also signed up with the SS. Hügel had a mind that leant itself to intelligence work and he was called up to the SD in September 1939, where he worked at sending agents into Switzerland. He went back to the civil service just three months later and then in June 1940 enlisted with the Luftwaffe. However, Hügel suffered an ear drum injury after just three weeks and was invalided out. He spent the next few years working at the RSHA headquarters, where he was put in charge of stoking racial tensions in Switzerland by secretly directing their right-wing parties for the Amt VI.

Klaus Hügel was part of a Nazi security apparatus that was as bureaucratic and complex as it was ruthless and sadistic — a system that also offered plenty of opportunities for corruption and rivalries to flourish, as we shall see. The various wings of the German state security system were brought under the auspices of the Reich Main Security Office (RSHA) in September 1939. Headed up by Reinhard Heydrich, this formally combined the Sicherheitsdienst (SD), the intelligence service of the SS, with the Sicherheitspolizei (SiPo), the Security Police, which until then had been under the jurisdiction of the Interior Ministry. Within the SiPo, which was dissolved, were two main sub-departments, the Geheime Staatspolizei (generally known as the Gestapo, the Secret State Police) and the Kriminalpolizei (KriPo, the police for ordinary criminal affairs). Within the basic structure of the RSHA, the organization at its simplest was divided into seven offices, or Ämter. Crucial to Anja's story was the Amt VI, the foreign intelligence wing of the SD, or Ausland-SD, for which both she and Klaus Hügel worked.

The system was sprawling and chaotic, and each department operated with a large degree of autonomy and dozens of local branches. The SD also served as the intelligence branch for the Gestapo, and in the occupied territories was coordinated locally by high-ranking SS inspectors. These local branches of the SD, Kripo and Gestapo would often work together very closely — but sometimes also as rivals. Corruption was rife, with many officials on the ground finding they had the freedom to cook up their own money-making schemes. As we shall see, Anja soon found herself in the midst of such people.

Anja must have been aware that the overarching mission of the RSHA and all its subdivisions, including the Ausland-SD, was the persecution and murder of Europe's Jews. For example, one of the main architects of the Holocaust, Adolf Eichmann, was head of the Amt IV (Suppression of Opposition) sub-department Referat IV B4, which organised the categorization and deportation of millions of Jews to the gas chambers and concentration camps. It was also his Reich Association of Jews in Germany that tricked Jewish families, such as the Götz women, into selling their property in exchange for living quarters, food and medical care in the Theresienstadt ghetto. The RSHA also oversaw the SS Einsatzgruppen death squads that were originally formed by Heydrich out of the SD, Gestapo, Kripo, and Waffen-SS. These groups were estimated to have killed more than two million people over the course of the war.

It's also worth noting, as we consider Anja's decision to undertake espionage work for this organization, the wider context of the period. In January 1943, Himmler had ordered the dissolution of the Warsaw Ghetto. At the time, 40,000 Jews were still living there, and Himmler wanted at least 8,000 deported within days. The action led to an uprising in April and the deaths of thousands of Nazis, much to the surprise and dismay of the leadership. Then, on May 21, 1943, Himmler had ordered all Jews from Reich territory to be deported, either to Theresienstadt or 'the east', an ominous directive that meant only one thing — death.

Himmler had taken personal charge of the RSHA after Heydrich was assassinated in May 1942, but when he became Reich Minister of the Interior in July 1943 — several weeks after meeting Anja — he appointed SS-Obergruppenführer Ernst Kaltenbrunner in his place. Kaltenbrunner was a fanatical Austrian Nazi with deep facial scars, supposedly from dueling, who counted Walter Schellenberg, Himmler's choice to head the Ausland-SD, as an enemy.

Partly as a result of the staunch Jewish fightback in the Warsaw ghetto, the SS began to ramp up the dissolution of all Polish ghettos, leading to the murder of some 80,000 people between May and the end of June. By the start of July, there were only about 30,000 Jews still living in the General Government area, most of them in labour camps, but Himmler demanded that "the evacuation of the Jews must be carried out ruthlessly and must be got through despite the unrest that will occur during the next three to four months as a result". Himmler, with Hitler's permission, declared the region a "bandit combat area" clearing the way for all sorts of extra-judicial killings. Over this period, the RSHA also organised the mass murder in Auschwitz of some 45,000 Jews deported from Saloniki, Greece, between March and August 1943.

While the Nazis were, from their point of view, successful with anti-Jewish measures in most of the occupied territories, they hit a road block in Italy. Unlike other areas under Nazi control, the nation was an ally and not a conquest, and did not support, at least in full, Hitler's racist policies. Even when, for example, German and Italian troops occupied southern France together in November 1942, the Italians were not prepared to help with deportations. They also refused to implement the Vichy Government order that Jews must wear the yellow Star of David and in fact allowed to Jews to migrate from the German zone. Similar beneficence was shown by the Italians towards Jews in Greece and Yugoslavia. And while back home Mussolini had reluctantly introduced laws to persecute Italy's Jews, antisemitism was not popular in Italy. Most people had no problem with the country's relatively small Jewish population. Mussolini, even while trying to appease his German allies, drew the line at deportations.

This presented a serious problem for Himmler, who complained that the Italian attitude provided "the excuse for many circles in France and throughout Europe to stall over the Jewish question because they can point out that not even our Axis partner is prepared to cooperate". Himmler worried that this was having a knock-on effect in Croatia, Romania, Bulgaria and Slovakia, and Himmler "urgently" appealed to the Italian Foreign Minister. Everything changed on July 25, 1943, when Mussolini was ousted from power and arrested. Six weeks later, on September 8, Italy signed an Armistice with the Allies and tens of thousands of German forces moved in to seize the northern and central areas, springing Mussolini from jail and having him declare the formation of the Italian Social Republic.

Until this point, the Ausland-SD in Italy had been restricted because spying was officially banned under the Axis agreement. But now, SD spies working with SS and Gestapo killers began to root out the country's Jews. Once the occupation began, it took just two weeks for Himmler to telegraph the following order to Herbert Kappler, head of Rome's Gestapo: "Recent events in Italy make it necessary that a final solution is found to the Jewish problem in the territories occupied by the armed forces of the Reich." Actions against the 8,000 Jews of Rome were to be carried out "quickly and secretly," he added.[40]

Hotels near the Swiss border began to swell with wealthy Jews from Milan and Turin. Himmler ordered the SS to round them up and pilfer their suitcases, which were filled with currency, jewellery and fake papers. At least forty nine men, women and children were summarily executed and their bodies left floating in Lake Maggiore.

Kappler later told his war crimes trial that he had not wanted to deport Jews from Italy, and that there was "no Jewish problem" in the country, as there was in Germany. But the truth was that Kappler was a rabid antisemite and he was simply not keen to carry out the operation because he lacked resources — and the subsequent public outcry was sure to cause him more problems. The head of the German military in Italy, Field Marshal Albert Kesselring, refused to free up troops to help, so Kappler conceived a plan to appease Hitler and Himmler.

Kappler went to the heads of Rome's Jewish community and demanded blood money — if fifty kilograms of gold were not delivered to him, two hundred Jews would be deported. The amount was duly raised and taken to the German Embassy, under police escort. And while Kappler's officers behaved badly, disputing the weights and refusing to give a receipt, Kappler promised that Rome's Jews would be safe. But the next morning, SS and Gestapo forces raided the city's main synagogue, relieving it of two million lire and half its library. Kappler's thugs also seized a complete list of Rome's Jewish families. Many began to flee their homes.

Frustrated with the delay, Himmler once again ordered the complete extermination of Rome's Jews, and Eichmann sent SS Captain Theodor Dannecker to carry out the mission. Dannecker was duly given the list of names by Kappler, and on October 16, 1943, SS thugs rounded up 1,259 Jews and non-Aryans and brought them in trucks to the Collegio Militare. Baptized Christians were later released, but 1,041 men, women and children were put on a train to Auschwitz. Only fifteen survived the war. Most perished in the gas chambers.

The pogrom was by no means the last atrocity to be inflicted on Italy's Jewish population. On December 1, the interior minister Buffarini Guidi issued the following statement to the press: "All Jews living on the national territory are to be arrested no matter what nationality they are. All their goods are to be sequestered by the State for the benefit of the poor. Those Jews who are of mixed birth will be placed under special surveillance." However, he delayed the publication of the statement for twenty-four hours to allow the news to leak out and give as many Jews as possible the chance to go into hiding.

But by the time Rome was liberated on June 4, 1944, the city's Fascist chief of police had handed over nearly 1,200 Jews to the Nazis. Thousands of Jews were placed in concentration camps on Italian soil, often in transit before being sent to Auschwitz. To their credit, many Italian politicians and public servants were in step with the majority public opinion and opposed the persecution. As a result, thousands of lives were probably saved through non-cooperation and foot-dragging. Still, out of some 32,000 Italian Jews, plus some 12,500 foreigners, 7,682 were killed. Of the 8,369 who were deported, only 979 came home.[41]

By April 1944, large parts of upper and central Italy were added to the raft of Himmler's "bandit combat areas," allowing the Nazis to carry out all manner of extra-judicial killings, including the Fosse Ardeatine Massacre, just outside Rome, in which German forces under Kappler's command executed 335 people, mostly Italians, in reprisal for a partisan attack on an SS police unit that killed thirty-three. Kappler had been the chief organiser of the atrocity and shot at least one victim himself. Incidentally, a Captain Koehler was also involved in the massacre and scouted out the location for the slaughter.[42]

Clearly a valued officer in the SD, Klaus Hügel rose through the ranks and in March 1944 was posted to Italy. He was put in charge of the Ausland-SD's Verona branch, where he later came into contact with Anja, several months after her husband had been captured, and almost a year since her meeting with Heinrich Himmler. In all that time, nothing that the Nazis had done in her adopted homeland, or elsewhere, had persuaded her not to spy for Himmler. In fact, Hügel told his MI5 interrogators that Kappler was one of many Nazi war criminals who Anja Manfredi got to know well.

***

Baron Manfredi had been unable to furnish his interrogators with details of his wife's secret activities. He had, after all, been captured in October 1943, just a few months after Anja met with Himmler, and he was only released after the war. But Klaus Hügel was a different matter and his statement, included as an appendix in Baron Manfredi's MI5 file, is the only fully intact account of Anja's espionage activities available to the public. While it therefore must be treated with some caution, the basic narrative and timeline is backed up by fragments to be found in surviving OSS files on Nazis in Italy released by the US National Archives.

Hügel's account of Anja's meeting with the SS-Reichsführer referred to Anja's collapse as a "fainting fit," adding that, "Himmler happened to be there and rendered assistance". In his opinion, Anja had "managed to take advantage of this brief acquaintance" and, sometime in early 1944, on Himmler's direct orders, Amt VI (the Ausland-SD) "had to take her over for Intelligence work". On the one hand, Hügel was doubtful as to whether the nature of the relationship between Anja and Himmler was physical, yet Anja certainly gave the impression that there had been a romantic development:

> [Baroness] Manfredi was only too willing to talk of her acquaintance with Himmler and her description of this was such that the listener gained the impression it had been of an intimate nature. On the other hand, she would speak so fulsomely of her immense respect for Heinrich Himmler (she invariably used both Christian and surname) as a man and a

politician, that one's first impression faded. Her physical appearance, which, despite all the cosmetic arts, remained that of a somewhat well-worn forty, and her excited and hysterical manner, did not tend to make her a very attractive woman, so it would not appear likely that Himmler had found her pleasing. But then, if one only considers those of her successes with men of which I have knowledge (certainly only a fraction of the total) it is nevertheless proof that she must have possessed strong powers of attraction.

Hügel did not elaborate on the number or identity of Anja's other lovers, but photographs show that she was hardly unattractive, certainly no less appealing than Himmler's rather unfit wife. It was well within the bounds of possibility that Himmler had found Anja "pleasing".

Hügel explained that Anja's spying career had begun very shortly after her return to Rome in July 1943, where she was initially controlled by Herbert Kappler. However, Kappler left no known record of any specific missions that Anja might have undertaken during this period.

Shortly after the Allied invasion in September — when Baron Manfredi was trying to arrange passage for his wife to Switzerland — Anja was moved to a hotel in Genoa, from where she funneled a few "minor reports" directly to Himmler via Kappler. The choice of Genoa might have been strategic from the German point of view, it being one of Italy's most important port cities. On the other hand, it was also just 20km from Rapallo, giving Anja easy access to her son. Clearly, she wanted to keep Aldo close. In return for the reports to Himmler, Anja repeatedly asked the head of the SS in the Ligura region, another war criminal, Freidrich Engel, to be sent on an espionage mission to Switzerland. This was where Hügel came in.

In March 1944, when Klaus Hügel arrived in Verona, it fell to him to make an assessment of Anja's prospects as an agent in the field. Apparently without meeting her, he delivered a harsh verdict:

Although she had no experience of any kind, she was nevertheless convinced that she possessed unusual talent for intelligence work. But closer investigation gave an unfavorable picture of Manfredi's personal qualifications. In fact, she could offer no contacts in Switzerland worth mentioning, beyond a well-known surgeon who she wished to perform an abdominal operation on her and a professor of music from whom she proposed to take lessons. I therefore refused to employ her.

Anja's career seemed to have stalled. While the meeting with Himmler had given Anja instant access to some of Italy's leading Nazis, it had not gotten her past the watchful eye of Klaus Hügel. And perhaps he was right to doubt her.

We will probably never know how deeply, if at all, Anja sympathized with the evil creed of Nazism, or whether she was really playing a deeper game. On the one hand, it's hard to see how Anja could have befriended and negotiated with this cadre of committed Nazis if she had not become one herself. At the time, several of her former in-laws were being murdered in concentration camps. Although she might not have known the details, she was must have been aware that the Götz family had been persecuted and there is no indication that she tried to have them freed.

Then again, there is little in Anja's background to suppose that she agreed in any way with the goals or anti-Jewish philosophy of the regime. Firstly, Anja had married a man of Jewish ancestry, very much in the face of opposition from her antisemitic father. Furthermore, even though she and her second husband, Baron Manfredi, were on friendly terms with many Germans, they also had Jewish friends who continued to socialise with them even at the height of the war. Furthermore, Anja's opposition to the bombing of London had also been flagged as suspicious by the OVRA, who since 1934 had believed her to be a Russian spy.

The most obvious answer was Anja's need to protect Aldo. Everybody knew that she had a half-Jewish son who she wanted to have 'Aryanised'. At any moment, men such as Kappler, Engel, Hügel or even Himmler himself, could have ordered Aldo, and Anja, to be arrested and deported to a concentration camp. It's clear that Himmler held Anja in high regard, because she became increasingly vocal about fulfilling her goal, and perhaps her insistence at being sent on a mission was a way to reinforce this trust and protect her imperiled offspring.

But not everyone was as trusting as Himmler, and it was not only Klaus Hügel who wished to block her path. Italian suspicions about Anja's true allegiances remained, even after her meeting with the SS-Reichsführer and several months into her service for the Nazis. Indeed, the bad smell persisted until, in the summer of 1944, Anja was again arrested by the Italian police on suspicion of espionage, much to Hügel's delight.

This time however, Anja's detention had been ordered by the local branch of the Abwehr, Germany's military intelligence service. Klaus Hügel caught wind of the arrest and felt "glad that my decision had proved to be correct". The Abwehr's chief concern was Anja's "many and constantly changing contacts with German officers". There was also the matter of a musical manuscript which she claimed to have written, but which was deemed by experts to be unplayable. Anja claimed she wanted to take it with her to Switzerland to help with her "musical studies," but German military spooks feared a code was hidden in the document.

For most foreigners arrested in Italy on espionage charges, this would have been the end. If summary execution was avoided, then the prisoner's most likely fate would be deportation to a concentration camp and either immediate murder, or execution at some point in the near future. Anja's situation was particularly dire — having been protected several times in the past thanks to her husband's impeccable contacts, she was now completely alone. If she was killed, he would not even know about it. Anja no doubt assumed her son would be arrested next, and there was no question of the fate that awaited him as a Jew. But Anja was in a unique position. Of all the suspected spies rounded up by the Nazis in their occupied territories, she was alone in having cultivated a personal relationship with the head of the SS itself — the second most powerful man in Nazi Germany.

According to Hügel, Anja launched an immediate appeal to Himmler. What happened next is not fully clear. But in the wake of the July 20, 1944, plot to assassinate the Führer, Hitler had signed a decree abolishing the Abwehr, fearing it was overrun with defectors and Allied spies, and at the time of Anja's arrest the organisation in Italy was in the process of being absorbed by the SD. In other words, the case fell into Hügel's lap and, by extension, those of Amt VI chief Walter Schellenberg and Himmler.

An extensive report was written for Himmler's perusal, which found the reasons for Anja's arrest were "unsound". The directive came back — Anja was to be released. Hügel didn't say who wrote the report, or whether it had been intended to clear Anja from the outset. He also didn't say precisely what the evidence was against her. Clearly, whatever the Abwehr had on her, Himmler wasn't convinced. Anja was released but, as we shall see, the Baroness later gave an entirely different account of her arrest and period of detention.

Even though Himmler was clearly in her corner, Hügel still doubted Anja's suitability for espionage, citing her "way of life," and refused to give her an assignment. Later, when being questioned by Allied forces, Anja remembered things differently. She claimed that while in Verona in May 1944, Hügel asked her to go to Florence, where she was to wait until the city was overrun and then begin spreading anti-Russian propaganda. Anja insisted that she refused this mission. If it happened at all, this was most probably a ploy by the frustrated Hügel to get her off his back.

Hügel said that after Anja was released she took a trip to Berlin, either in July or August 1944. Hügel did not know what she did there, but almost immediately upon her arrival back in Italy, he was handed a directive by Schellenberg in no uncertain terms: give Baroness Manfredi anything she needs. In Hügel's view: "It amounted to the carrying out of a personal order from Himmler, for the success of which I was to be responsible."

Forced into a corner, Hügel decided to meet with Anja in person. The pair spoke for hours and Hügel did his best to persuade Anja that that her espionage plans would go nowhere. Hügel said her "strongest counter-argument was always her feminine charm which she intended to use successfully on British and American diplomats in Switzerland". "It was quite impossible to argue with her," he added.

Thoroughly dejected by her persistence, Hügel arranged for Anja to move to Milan — Genoa was no longer safe for her because of the common knowledge that she was friends with Himmler — and told her to apply for a Swiss entry visa. Anja was finally getting her way. A few weeks later, Anja informed Hügel that she wished to travel once again to Berlin to see Himmler, before going to Switzerland. Hügel checked, and Anja was indeed expected at Himmler's personal office, as well as at the Amt-VI headquarters in Berlin. How was it that this strange woman, who until a few months previously had been suspected of being an enemy agent, was now able to dictate when and where she would visit with top level officials in Germany? Hügel was growing increasingly concerned.

In a last-ditch effort to stop Anja in her tracks, and risking the wrath of both Himmler and Schellenberg, Hügel wrote a memo to Berlin in which he strongly advised employing Anja in the Red Cross, or some other organisation inside Germany, rather than send her on an espionage mission. Anja nevertheless made her journey to Berlin in October or November 1944. Hügel said he then heard that Anja was in Innsbruck, waiting for transport back to Italy. But because he received no direct orders from Berlin he didn't send a car, leaving her stranded. It was a spiteful and passive-aggressive show of non-compliance, but it gave Hügel some satisfaction, as well as a break from Anja's demands.

A few days later, Hügel received furious telegrams from two adjutants attached to Himmler's office. They repeated the order to send Anja to Switzerland and "afford her all possible aid," including in matters unrelated to her mission. One letter was "addressed to me personally and was in an unusually sharp tone," Hügel recalled. This letter, from war criminal Eugen Steimle, a former commander in the Einsatzgruppen, said the mission to Switzerland was "regarded in the Amt as exceedingly propitious, whereas we in Italy were prejudiced against her".

Hügel said that when Anja eventually found her way back to Italy and tracked him down in Verona, she was "full of triumph and boasted of how marvelously she had been received everywhere in Berlin". As Hügel recalled: "Her demands and her behaviour in Italy were now as might have been expected".

This was quite a remarkable turn of events. From a supposedly chance meeting in a restaurant, Anja was now able to bend one of the most powerful men in Nazi Germany to her will, demand personal meetings at his office and instigate reprimands to relatively senior SD figures such as Hügel. It was beyond belief, but perhaps Hügel should have had more faith in Anja's "feminine charms". Still, Hügel questioned whether or not Anja had actually been granted a personal audience with Himmler during her visit to Berlin. He felt that Anja had "cleverly avoided" answering any questions about the subject. Instead, Hügel felt, she had won another of his aides, Martin Fälschlein, over to her side. In any case, Anja's victory over Hügel left her full of beans. She was handed 100,000 lire and was due to receive a further 3,000 Swiss Francs. Both sums, Hügel felt, were "unusually high", but this was what the boss wanted. There was an agreement to send further, regular payments, once Anja reached Switzerland.

By now, Aldo was working for a German company based in Milan. Having been handed a huge sum of cash for her Switzerland trip, Anja made a further demand to Hügel that her son be Aryanised as soon as possible. This task fell under the remit of the directive from Berlin, she insisted.

As Anja prepared to leave Genoa for Milan, the German and Italian authorities both wanted to search her luggage, but she refused and as usual emerged from the blazing row victorious. Most suspiciously, she insisted on holding on to her bizarre musical manuscript. Had the Abwehr's fears about Anja's loyalty been well-founded? Was she secretly batting for either the Allies, the Russians, or Finland? If so, somebody had successfully infiltrated an agent into a position of influence at the very highest reaches of the Nazi state.

In any case, Klaus Hügel could now breathe a sigh of relief — Anja was no longer his direct problem. Once settled in Milan, as she awaited her papers for the mission to Switzerland, Anja was to be handled by an SD man who, despite his involvement in the evils of the regime, was a Nazi of quite a different stripe to the charmless, suspicious, and loyal Klaus Hügel. Anja's new handler was flamboyant, promiscuous, deeply corrupt and, above all, a traitor.

---

[39] Hügel files, UK National Archives.
[40] Lamb, p.39.
[41] Lamb, p.55.
[42] See Katz, Death in Rome.

A Nest of Spies

Guido Zimmer was in his early 30s and easy on the eye. Blue-eyed, athletic, medium height and with blonde hair, greying at the temples, his secretary and lover Lydia Flügel described him as having an "elegant bearing" and a "cheerful disposition". Zimmer was said to have a large mouth and prominent teeth, and spoke in a rather high-pitched voice. He was also a terribly incompetent spy.

Zimmer was born in Westphalia in November, 1911, and began his working life in 1931 as an apprentice with the Hamburg import and export company Siemssen and Co, a similar business to the one that had made Hans Götz's father a very wealthy man, in that very same city.[43] Zimmer later worked as an intern at the Wolff's Telegraphisches Bureaux in Munich and Berlin, learning trade communications. The organisation was nationalised by the Nazis, shortly after Zimmer joined the party in 1932. Zimmer later helped to set up a factory for another company in Berlin between 1933 and 1936, before joining the SS. He began his training in theoretical counter-espionage in Berlin in 1937 and in 1940 went to work in the RSHA, Amt VI — foreign intelligence.

Zimmer's first assignment was a disaster. Transferred to Rome in 1940, where he worked under Herbert Kappler, he moved into an apartment in Via Gasparo Spontini, whose last tenants had been Russian diplomats forced to flee at the outbreak of war. He told the maid, Rosa Cappelli, that he was a journalist. But Zimmer blew his own cover by passing on a piece of what he considered vital information to an Italian contact rather than his own superiors. This exposed his true purpose in Rome and he was recalled to Berlin under a cloud. Zimmer was only spared from being dismissed in disgrace by the intervention of an influential uncle. His apartment was taken over by a friend who the maid had seen visit many times, alongside high-ranking Nazis and diplomats. The man's name was Koehler.

Zimmer languished in Berlin for the next three years, but when Mussolini was overthrown in September 1943 the RSHA needed bodies to throw at the territory — Italy had to be occupied and held at all costs and, now the opportunity had arisen, the Jews of Italy could be dealt with. Zimmer soon found himself in Genoa, working under Klaus Hügel. Then, in April 1944, he was transferred to Milan to set up a special SD unit, working under the command of Standartenführer Walter Rauff, Chief of the Security Police and SD in North West Italy.

Rauff was one of the most twisted Nazis active in the country at the time. Previously, he had been integral in designing a way to ease the 'burden' placed on SS men engaged in mass shootings of Jews and other prisoners — the gas van. Rauff supervised the modification of trucks so that exhaust fumes would be diverted into airtight chambers in the back, where up to sixty people at a time could be murdered. SS-Obersturmführer Zimmer was never involved in anything so barbaric, but he did have a dual role in Milan — firstly to build up a network or post-occupational agents, and also to rid the area of Jews. Rauff gave Zimmer a long leash and the wayward spy took full advantage by giving himself a third objective — personal enrichment.

He soon found himself in like-minded company. Shortly before Zimmer arrived in Italy, a group of SS men led by the notorious director of the Gestapo-run San Vittore prison, Theodor Saeveke, took over a villa in Milan's Via Marengo after seizing it from a Jewish family. Saeveke was a sadistic killer implicated in several massacres and dozens of summary executions, as well as the deportations of hundreds of Jews. He was also the go-to man for any Nazi official looking for a place to live in the city. Saeveke's new apartment was already filled with filled with art, jewels and silverware looted from Jewish homes and synagogues, and there was no space for Zimmer. But Saeveke's mob commandeered another Jewish villa on Via Domenico Cimarosa and Zimmer duly moved in with his secretary. This shows that whatever else Zimmer might later have done for the partisans and the Allies, there is no escaping the fact that he benefitted, right from the start, as a result of Jewish persecution. Zimmer and Saeveke were not exactly neighbours, but with just over a mile between the two apartments, the Gestapo man would be able to keep an eye on the spy, and vice-versa.

Zimmer was gleefully corrupt and — while he had a chequered history as a spy — he had an eye for business. As one captured Nazi collaborator later put it, Zimmer and his gang were "doing little work and spent most of their time in good living". Sensing that Germany was inevitably going to lose the war, Zimmer had no qualms about lining his own pockets and made friends with well-connected Italians who felt the same. One of these partners in the sale of black market goods was Baron Luigi Parilli, by chance another member of the Knights of Malta.

Alongside dealing on the black market and looting Jewish homes, Zimmer came up with a novel line in springing arrested Italians, even those interned in Germany. His usual method was to insist that the individual was merely posing as an enemy agent and that they were in fact working for him. The ploy seemed to work most of the time. Zimmer would later highlight these acts as an example of his benevolence during the war, although somehow they only ever seemed to involve people from wealthy families.

Zimmer also knew the location of treasure stolen from the French in Africa, worth millions of Francs, and was waiting to use the proceeds to finance his stay-behind agents. It was hidden somewhere between Como and Varese, and was still being hunted by French spies after the war.

More than likely, Zimmer had kept the loot hidden, gambling on the prospect that Germany would be defeated and he could keep it for himself.

Zimmer often played host to Saeveke and his goons, and occasionally had his wife and child stay with him. But at most other times his home was frequented by a succession of lovers, including at least one long-term Dutch mistress. He also became friendly with a group of Italian partisans and used his connections to save Colonel Minetti of the Gruppo D'Annunzio from execution by an SS firing squad in Parma. Although Zimmer had no direct influence there, he was able to "bluff" the rebel to freedom. He also helped to free another arrested partisan named Decio, by claiming he was an agent and was merely playing the part of an anti-fascist. The ploy worked but the man was later arrested again in Turin, and Zimmer could do nothing.

In addition, Zimmer claimed he tried to help a German citizen of Jewish descent named Ursula Altmann, by saying he aimed to recruit her fiancé, the owner of a Turin radio company. Zimmer was able to prevent her arrest on several occasions and a report about his conduct went back to Gestapo HQ. Luckily for him, the investigation seemed to fizzle out.

Zimmer must have got a thrill from the double risk of being caught cheating by his wife and being arrested by the ever-watchful Saeveke. But his treacherous dealings with the partisans went much further than the occasional rescue operation. He began to help militiamen obtain false identification papers and also "offered his services formally" to the National Liberation Committee, the umbrella organisation for the Italian resistance. Zimmer even preemptively informed Colonel Minneti of the "coming capitulation," so that resistance forces could begin to mobilize, and then asked for help to broach negotiations with the Allies. If Saeveke had got wind of this betrayal, the committed Nazi would have had him shot on the spot. But he would also have been stunned to discover that Zimmer's treachery was not an isolated case, and in fact extended to the very top of the SS.

Zimmer's primary purpose in Milan was not hunting Jews and he had little appetite for the work, besides the opportunities it presented for profiteering. His main focus, officially, was on setting up a post-occupational network of spies and saboteurs who could oppose both the Allies and partisans in the inevitable event that the entire country was overrun. This he achieved with some success.

One of Zimmer's most promising agents was the Countess Savorgnani, who intended to set up a trucking firm in Milan as cover. She had a tragic back story — born as a result of an illicit affair, she was raised by her much older half-brother, who posed as her father, and was married off into the aristocracy at the age of seventeen. Enduring an unhappy marriage, her brother and only child were killed in an Allied airstrike in Trieste in April 1944. She became mistress to another SS man, Walter Segna, and later, when officials in Italy were secretly planning to surrender, she was offered up by Segna as a possible conduit to open talks with the Allies, although ultimately the plan didn't bear fruit.

Another of Zimmer's agents was the Yugoslavian Miodrag Jevremovic, unimaginatively codenamed Draga. Zimmer praised Draga in his notebook as a "very energetic individual" who prepared his own fake passports and other documents ahead of time while waiting to embark on a mission to see his existing handlers in Germany. This impressed Zimmer, who said he had "accomplished more in a few days than an agent of average attainments could do in weeks and months," and expressed an intention to sign him up for his own team. Draga was kept waiting in Germany for nearly a month before being dispatched back to Italy — with a weak cover story and without the 50,000 lire he had been promised. With just twenty-four lire in his pocket, Zimmer said Draga had had his "will crushed". The spy threw in the towel with his intelligence organisation and signed up with Zimmer's unit.

Draga was as daring as he was industrious. On one undercover mission inside the Spanish consul in Milan, he succeeded in getting the keys to the vault all to himself for forty minutes. In this time, he made an impression in wax, given to him "in great haste" by Zimmer, and a master key was made. Photographs were later taken of the most sensitive documents stored inside. Draga's mistress was also involved in the plot, and was sleeping with the Spanish consul-general in a bid to expose a German double-agent.

One of Zimmer's most surprising recruits was Andreas Zolyomy, a Hungarian Jew and star water polo player who went on to take part in seven Olympic game as both competitor and coach. Zimmer described agent Andreas as a "well-known sportsman" who was "very capable and courageous". Andreas "found plain intelligence very irksome" and made his own way to Switzerland out of boredom after working for the SIM in Naples. Zimmer sought him out and recruited him. Posing as a Communist, Andreas set up a rebel cell in Milan, numbering some twenty-six operatives. The aim was to have just enough members to become a legitimate force within the Communist Party and then to erode it from within. Zimmer's unit made sure they were well stocked with guns and grenades.

Zimmer had no time for turncoats within his own camp. His notes mentioned an agent who volunteered to go with two others on a mission to purchase 600 gold coins. He asked for 1.32m lire and entered the apartment alone, leaving the other men at the door, as requested. They were to come in five minutes later, but found the agent had used a side door to escape with the money. Zimmer ordered him to be arrested and deported to a concentration camp, adding: "The man is simply a thief."

It was a life of constant intrigue and threat. Spies were captured or escaped, Zimmer always suspected double dealing, and was wary of agents who were working for his colleagues, ostensibly in other parts of the country. Zimmer had a particular interest in industrial espionage and was obsessed with cultivating informants inside motor companies and trucking firms, including Fiat, Lancia and Alfa Romeo, whose chief engineer Wilfredo Riccard, became an agent. In one case, this helped him identify a worker suspected of helping the Allies plan an airstrike on the plant where he worked. But Zimmer was clearly also planning for life after the war, and intended to spend his time making friends in useful places.

Anja Manfredi was also among Zimmer's cohort, but she was not a spy of the same type as Draga or Andreas. It was impossible for her to work deep undercover — she was simply to brash and boastful of her connections to Himmler. Indeed, when Zimmer's boss Walter Rauff was eventually captured he gave up a huge amount of intelligence on RSHA operations inside Italy, but did not categorise Anja as a member of Zimmer's post-occupational network, merely calling her an "informer". That being said, other mere "informers" on Rauff's list included Baron Parilli, and some other very high-level operatives, perhaps suggesting that Rauff did not know everything that Zimmer was working on.[44]

But Anja certainly had her uses in Milan and undertook at least one or two minor missions for Zimmer while waiting to go to Switzerland, although he did not record their exact nature. It was agreed that Anja would stay at the Hotel Plaza and not show her face at Zimmer's Milan office for reasons of secrecy, but she disregarded this order and repeatedly turned up to speak with him, making frequent personal demands, as well as some mission suggestions. For example, according to Zimmer's diaries — which were sporadic, written in German shorthand and later translated by the Americans — Anja suggested that she could seduce and turn a leading partisan to the Nazi cause. "Her newest brainchild is to woo the Communist leader PARI (sic) to our purposes as an agent. Only release from the local jail would allegedly be necessary," he wrote.

Anja's proposed task would have been far more difficult than she hoped. Ferrucio Parri was one of the top military planners in the resistance, had long been working for the Americans, and would become Italy's first post-war Prime Minister. As Allen Dulles, the leading OSS man in Switzerland, later revealed, Parri had been cooperating with the Allies, via a system of secret couriers, and occasionally by risking his own life with a visit to Switzerland in person. According to Dulles' account, in late 1944, "at a time when partisan morale particularly needed bolstering," Parri was flown to the Allied base in Caserta, after sneaking into Switzerland and then into France. In Caserta, the Committee for the Liberation of Northern Italy (CLNAI) was given official Allied partner status and handed responsibility for maintaining law and order once the Germans pulled out. Unfortunately, upon his return Parri was arrested in a round-up of resistance members and detained in Milan's Hotel Regina.

Fellow partisans disguised in SS uniforms tried to free him in a daring raid after entering through a skylight from a neighbouring roof, but Parri was intercepted by guards, badly beaten and moved to an SS-run prison in Verona.

Given the context, it's interesting that Anja suggested freeing Parri, and it remains the only example of an occasion where she seemingly tried to spring someone from custody.

Another entry in Zimmer's diary suggests that Himmler was issuing direct orders to Anja, noting that the proposed trip to Switzerland "was ordered personally by the RFM". Referring to another, unidentified, mission, Zimmer said Anja "did not wish the RFM to know about her SD assignment". This was apparently because Himmler was willing to pay her expenses for a trip to Switzerland for health purposes. However, Zimmer wrote, "She says that she belongs to that class of people who do not want anything for nothing; therefore she had offered to work for [the] office." In the same note, Zimmer also referred to a previous mission, in which Anja had "obtained results in a very important case".

Although Zimmer believed that Anja did have the connections to wealthy people of which she boasted, he was wary of her. On one occasion, she claimed to have been robbed and, as a result, was handed a further 80,000 lire. She also asked for a sum of money to retrieve diamonds and chains left on her account at her hotel and worth, Anja claimed, another 80,000 lire. Zimmer wrote about these incidents, saying of the robbery that, "Two days before she had told me that she did not have any more money." He wrote begrudgingly to Berlin: "You are urged to send some money."

Still, Zimmer knew that Anja was in Milan awaiting transit on a personal mission to Switzerland — a direct order from the SS-Reichsführer. He didn't particularly care how much she pocketed from Nazi coffers or what she did in Milan.

Klaus Hügel was a little more scathing of her behavior in the city, later telling MI5: "She spoke everywhere quite openly of her connection with Himmler and the Sicherheitzpolizei and ignored every warning to be prudent. She lived in Milan at such a rate that it is probable she engineered the 'robbery' because she had run out of money."

Then a real disaster struck — Anja's visa application was rejected. Whatever Himmler wanted her to do in Switzerland would now be impossible. According to Zimmer's notebooks, Anja tried "other ways" to get into Switzerland, including some not-so-subtle bribery with a visa clerk, telling him it was "absolutely essential" that she should get to Switzerland because she had to "bring her jewellery to safety". The clerk, hoping to gain from it, promised he would try again.

But a second application made in January 1945 was also refused. "Since there has been a denial of the permit for the well-known reason [Anja's association with Himmler]," Zimmer wrote, "the projected trip cannot benefit Abt VI in any way, because even for entry permits there is a very rigid control." Walter Rauff also described the snafu, simply stating how Anja was sent on a "special mission" to Switzerland by Amt VI, but was refused a visa.[45]

Anja's failure to gain entry to Switzerland once again placed her in mortal danger. Klaus Hügel believed that Anja had spent her time in Milan associating with partisans. Given her handler Zimmer's own close connections with the resistance, it's entirely reasonable that Anja would also have come into their orbit. In fact, it's not beyond the realms of possibility that Zimmer either brought her in on his dealings with the rebels, or otherwise used her as a conduit. It might explain her keenness to get Parri out of prison. Anja had also begun to bug Zimmer about the Aryanisation of her son, and complained to Hügel that he was not helping. As a result, another high-ranking SS man, Wilhelm Harster, made a renewed plea to the RSHA hierarchy to remove Anja from Italy, given that the plan to have her installed in Switzerland was now hopeless.

Instead, Hügel received by courier an SS-made porcelain Jullteller, or teller-plate, to pass onto Anja from Himmler. Hügel recalled that this was a gift that Himmler would send "to any woman to whom he wished to show attention". Indeed, Himmler was known to send porcelain gifts, for example, he sent a candlestick to the wife of Otto Wächter, then the governor of Kracow, to make the birth of the couple's fifth child.[46] But the gift sent to Anja came with a note from Martin Fälschlein, the contents of which are unknown, and an inscription that implied some personal affection: "Der Deutchen mutter" (to the German mother). It also suggested that Himmler might not have been aware of Aldo's true heritage after all.

The phrase had echoes of an award the Nazis created to honour women who made an exceptional contribution to the state. Named *Ehrenkreuz der Deutschen Mutter*, or the Cross of the German Mother, recipients and their children were allowed to have no Jewish blood. Perhaps Anja had been promised the medal in return for successfully carrying out her mission. Alternatively, it's possible that Himmler was being ironic, although he was not famed for his sense of humour. In return, Anja handed over a gift for Hügel to send to Himmler. Hügel again risked Himmler's wrath by sending back a note admonishing Fälschlein for his "indiscretion".

Hügel did not see Anja again after February 16, 1945. He was ill with lung trouble of his own and could barely work. He did read a report from Harster at the end of March, written after a meeting with Schellenberg and Kaltenbrunner in Thuringia. This document, which has apparently not survived, seemed to shed some light on Himmler's intentions for Anja:

> [Harster's report] was to the effect that everything which had been reported to the Amt from Italy regarding Manfredi, to her disfavor, was nothing in comparison with what was known her about her in the Amt and by Himmler himself. Notwithstanding however, it was Himmler's wish that she should go to Switzerland. He thought it important that a woman like her, whose appearance and way of living was exactly the opposite of what the world regarded as the SS ideal, should appear abroad as an admirer of his.

Even by the time of his confession in Camp 020, Hügel still wasn't sure what to make of Anja, or Himmler's plans for her, which seemed to be to provoke some sort of "positive response" for Himmler in Switzerland. This, it seemed to Hügel, was "scarcely conceivable". He wondered whether there had been a larger scheme at play, a "special mission". The only other explanation, which he doubted, was that Himmler was offering Anja an escape to a neutral country on "humanitarian grounds". He added, "Himmler was not often given to such kindly gestures, particularly not where women were concerned."

Hügel did concede that with the "Utopian hopes" that Himmler, Kaltenbrunner and others "still nursed...as regards their personal chances and how utterly falsely they judged the Allied and Neutral world, I do believe it possible that Himmler hoped to gain some support for himself abroad by the ridiculous dispatch of the Baroness Manfredi to Switzerland." Hügel thought it clear that Anja enjoyed "playing the role of friend and admirer" to Himmler because it brought personal benefits that she would otherwise not have had. He had this final, pithy, observation to make of Anja:

> In judging the Baroness Manfredi, considerable stress should be laid on her really bad health. She believed, or at least played with the possibility, that she was faced with an early and sudden death. For this reason, she wanted to snatch everything possible from life. This may well be the reason she became an adventuress — one might almost say a swindler.

Hügel lamented the fact that the suspicions against Anja could not be proved, partly because she had been "impossible" to surveil in Milan. But why had Himmler really been so desperate to send Anja to Switzerland in the first place? As Hügel had been at pains to point out, it was unlikely to be for a mere public relations exercise. There were also far easier ways for her to receive medical treatment, not least at Himmler's SS clinic in Hohenlychen.

The key to understanding Anja's true role as Himmler's most secret spy lies with the frenzied but separate activities undertaken by her boss, Himmler, and her handler Guido Zimmer, in the final months of the war, as Hitler's most trusted henchmen planned to betray their Führer.

---

[43] Zimmer files.
[44] Rauff files.
[45] Rauff files.
[46] Sands, p.79.

Himmler the Traitor

By the autumn of 1943 most senior Nazis realised that Germany was certain to lose the war eventually. Only Hitler and his most fanatical acolytes were still convinced of victory. This begged the question of exactly how defeat would come about. Would a scorched earth policy be imposed across all German-controlled territory, or could Hitler's forces lay down their arms with a modicum of decency? An equally important issue facing those affiliated with the SS and RSHA in particular was how best to ensure they would not be held personally accountable for war crimes. While some resolved simply to commit suicide, others saw a more calculating way out — by helping to bring about peace with the Allies.

By January 1945, Heinrich Himmler was entrenched at the SS clinic in Hohenlychen, the sanctuary where each of his offspring, legitimate and otherwise, had been born. Now he was there alone, without his trusted masseur Felix Kersten, complaining of his familiar stomach problems. The SS-Reichsführer had not even made it home to his long-suffering wife for Christmas, phoning Margarete at their Lake Tegernsee chalet in place of seeing her in person.

Himmler felt safest at the clinic — its roof was painted with a Red Cross symbol so that it wouldn't be bombed. He hoped it would never come to that, because for months he had been working on the ultimate insurance policy — making peace with Britain, America, and even the Jews.

Many claims have been made about exactly when, where and why Himmler began pursuing talks with the Western Allies, but at least since the middle of 1944 — and with the firm encouragement of his Ausland-SD spy chief Walter Schellenberg and therapist Felix Kersten, a de facto triple agent for Finland and Sweden — he had been making overtures about the release of certain Jews in return for war materials or foreign currencies. Himmler planned to use these dialogues to shift the focus onto ending the war, or at least onto persuading Britain and America to turn against the Russians.

The first successful deal of this nature took place after negotiations in Budapest between an SS delegation led by Eichmann and the Zionist Support and Rescue Committee, known as Vaada, in June 1944.[47] Around 15,000 Hungarian Jews were deported to a forced labour camp in Austria instead of to Auschwitz, a not particularly generous concession but a concession nonetheless. A further 1,684 victims were taken to Bergen-Belsen and then allowed to emigrate to Switzerland, all in exchange for 10,000 lorries needed by the Nazis. Further talks between the Germans and Jewish groups then took place on Swiss soil.

Himmler also personally held talks with Jean-Marie Musy, the former President of the Swiss Confederation, on two occasions — in October 1944, in Vienna, and in January 1945, in the Black Forest. As a result, 1,200 prisoners were allowed to leave Theresienstadt for Switzerland.

In an effort to improve his image, Himmler took sole responsibility for these actions, and boasted that Hitler only found out later, to his fury. But the fact was that Himmler had not recanted his antisemitism, and each and every move was a cynical ploy aimed at saving his own skin — at the same time that he was negotiating for the release of a few thousand victims, he was ordering the liquidation of concentration camps and the murder of tens of thousands of prisoners. But from early

1945, Himmler found fresh motivation to increase his contact with the Allies — he was fast falling out of favour with Hitler.

Himmler had further consolidated his power following the failed bid to assassinate the Führer on July 20, 1944. Even though Himmler himself might have been aware of the plot, he was the man charged with rounding up its key figures and other malcontents, the majority of whom had nothing to do with it. The black list eventually ran to some 5,000 names, many of them opponents or critics of the regime, as well as individuals who Himmler deemed a threat to him personally.

It was amid growing skepticism on Hitler's part about the loyalty of the Wehrmacht that Himmler was also appointed commander of the Reserve Army, giving him control of prisoners of war, the army penal system, and development of armaments. Next, he became commander-in-chief of the Army Group Upper Rhine, and was ordered to create the *Volkssturm* (People's Army) which aimed to conscript all German males aged sixteen to sixty, in the last desperate gambit of Goebbels' total war strategy. Hitler hoped this would bolster his forces by some six million men and stave off the Russian advance.

Himmler absorbed more military power in January 1945, when he became commander of the Army Group Vistula, which was charged with holding back the Soviet Red Army's offensive. Himmler was badly underqualified and spread too thin. When a disastrous German counter attack crumbled, Hitler humiliatingly stripped Himmler off his command. By the end of March 1945, with the walls closing in, Himmler knew that he would have to betray Hitler if he was to have any hope of surviving the coming defeat.

It was a bittersweet moment for the co-conspirators Felix Kersten and Walter Schellenberg, who had spent nearly three years trying to convince the vacillating Himmler to make a move on Hitler. Himmler, although aware of the Führer's poor health and mental instability, could never quite bring himself to put the wheels in motion.[48]

As a result of the talks that had begun in October 1944, in early February 1945, Himmler offered Musy the freedom of 3,500 Jews in exchange for asylum for himself and 200 leading Nazis. Himmler also wanted five million Swiss francs which he insisted would be transferred to the International Red Cross to provide relief for German civilians. The inmates would be sent to Switzerland in two trainloads. But after the first trainload of 1,700 Jews left Theresienstadt ghetto on February 8, Ernst Kaltenbrunner informed Hitler, who personally intervened to stop another 1,800 Jews from leaving Bergen-Belsen. It's not clear how Himmler survived this episode, but it did nothing to stop his overtures to the West.

On February 19, Himmler met with Count Folke Bernadotte, a Swedish nobleman and diplomat serving as Vice President of the Swedish Red Cross. The purpose of the meeting, which was partly facilitated by Kersten, was to discuss the release of Danish and Norwegian prisoners. The pair met again in early March and as a result some 8,000 Scandinavians and 13,000 other prisoners, including about 1,600 Jews, were freed from concentration camps via white buses painted with the Red Cross symbol. The so-called White Buses mission continued until the end of the war and beyond, when another 10,000 people were liberated. In truth, Himmler's only real motivation was to use Bernadotte to make overtures to the Western Allies.

Himmler and Hitler met for the final time on April 20, 1945, at a birthday party for the Führer, held in his Berlin bunker. Himmler was a reluctant attendee, fearing that he could be arrested, or worse. According to Kersten's account, Himmler told him that he'd spent some time at the party skulking in a corner with Hitler's doctor, Ludwig Stumpfegger, plotting to have the German dictator poisoned.[49]

The following day, Himmler compounded his treachery by meeting with Norbert Masur, the Swedish representative of the World Jewish Congress, to discuss the release of Jewish concentration camp inmates. Himmler used the occasion to tell a pack of lies about conditions at the camp and his own involvement in atrocities, stating that crematoria had only been built to handle the dead from a typhus epidemic. Masur bit his tongue throughout this horrifying encounter and secured the release of some 7,000 Jewish women from Ravensbrück.

On April 23, Himmler again met with Bernadotte, at the Swedish consulate in Lübeck. Perhaps buoyed by his pact with Hitler's doctor, Himmler insisted that the Führer would be dead within days and that he wanted to surrender to the Western Allies, rather than the Soviets. Himmler put the request in writing, as per Bernadotte's instruction. However, five days later, on the evening of April 28 — incidentally the same day that Allen Dulles was meeting with Italy's SS chiefs in Switzerland, as we shall see — Reuters circulated a news report about Himmler's attempt to open negotiations with Britain and America. This sent Hitler into an apoplectic rage and Himmler into a deep despair. It was at this moment of crisis that Himmler thought of Anja, and the record of this fact comes from a most unlikely source.

Walter Schellenberg had been the chief architect of Himmler's treachery, and it now seemed to him inevitable that he would be arrested and executed. Since November 1943, the Ausland-SD spy chief had been making overtures to the Western Allies through contacts in Stockholm and had grown close to Bernadotte during subsequent talks with the Swede. Now he believed the only way forward was to ramp up discussions by again going to Stockholm. Schellenberg enlisted Himmler's astrologist, Wilhelm Wulff, to convince the SS-Reichsführer that his stars showed the mission should go ahead. Wulff was duly dispatched to Lübeck, where Schellenberg greeted him with the words: "Make sure that Himmler sends me to Stockholm."[50]

As Wulff later wrote in his memoirs:

He [Schellenberg] looked very tired and worn; he was trembling as he took my hand and smiled to hide his fear. We then sat down in old basket chairs with filthy cushions and broken wickerwork which creaked every time we moved. The room in which we were sitting was musty and untidy and dimly lit. The dismal atmosphere made us even more aware of the misery around us. Schellenberg was deeply despondent, and I now discovered that it was he and not Himmler who had had me brought to Lübeck.

Schellenberg explained the situation, and added that in the wake of media attention the Western Allies were refusing to negotiate. As Wulff described it, Schellenberg was in a state of pure terror. "Himmler will accuse me of having placed him in an extremely difficult situation, because Hitler will now relieve him of his official posts. Everything is breaking down!" he said. According to Wulff, Himmler still believed that he could persuade the Western powers to join forces with him against the Russians and that "the Western powers would welcome him with open arms". Wulff added:

> When Schellenberg had finished speaking, I proposed that I should retire for an hour to study the various horoscopes and establish the answers to his questions in peace and quiet. Before meeting Himmler, I also wanted to memorize the new constellations which would be emerging in the immediate future. And after all the excitement and strain of the past few days, in which I had been constantly on the move, my mental and physical powers were at such a low ebb that I badly needed an hour of solitude. About an hour later I explained my proposals to Schellenberg. There were no indications in his horoscope that his life was then in danger, but there were signs of a forthcoming journey. Thus, I was able to advise him to prepare himself for a trip to Sweden and to think about who was to accompany him. After we had taken a light meal Schellenberg ordered his chauffeur to drive us to Himmler's command post.

Wulff described the disastrous state of the roads, which were littered with burnt out cars, and the refugees he encountered, who were stinking, despondent and exhausted. Soldiers stood around barking orders in a "scene of utter confusion". Finally, they reached a hut and, after some wait, Himmler arrived with a cigar stuffed in his mouth. He stank of booze and his face was swollen and flushed.

Himmler was distraught about the news reports and feared being arrested. He asked Wulff what his constellations had to say on the matter. Wulff spread out Himmler's horoscope and charts on the table, but was interrupted as Himmler recalled Wulff's previous advice to overthrow Hitler, and told him in a voice "in which agitation was mingled with regret": "I now realize, Herr Wulff, that in urging me to arrest Hitler and enter into peace negotiations through the English you were giving me honest advice. Now it is too late. Last year, when you warned me, the time was ripe. You meant well."

Himmler became more agitated, until he blurted out: "Now Hitler will have me arrested." Wulff tried to broach the issue of sending Schellenberg to Sweden, but the "overwrought and deathly pale" Himmler interrupted, repeating over and over again: "What's going to happen? What's going to happen? It's all over!" Wulff returned to the horoscope, insisting that Himmler "still had a chance," if he sent Schellenberg to Sweden for fresh talks with Bernadotte and the Swedish foreign minister. During these talks, he suggested, Himmler's own flight from Germany could be negotiated.

But at this point, Himmler announced his own, alternative plans. He discussed two options for himself, the first being that a member of his staff might hide him on his estate in Oldenburg. The second option was Anja. As Wulff wrote:

> There was a further possibility: A certain countess, half-Finnish and half-Italian, had once hinted that, if necessary, Himmler could go into hiding in Finland or Lapland. The countess was deeply indebted to Himmler, who had saved her son from execution. He liked her and had helped her on a number of occasions in her dealings with foreign authorities. This contact could now be followed up.

While Anja was a baroness and not a countess, the rest of the description matched her exactly. Anja was Finnish and naturalized Italian. Aldo had likely been spared deportation on Himmler's orders. And Himmler had done what he could for Anja, springing her from prison in Italy and pushing for her to get into Switzerland. Was this the real reason for Himmler's unwavering faith in the Baroness? That Anja had made an offer for Himmler to go into hiding on her land in Finland? If so, it was yet another swindle — Anja owned no known property there.

The rest of the conversation with Wulff was tense and rather dramatic, with Himmler sweating profusely and suffering from the shakes. Wulff insisted that he told him: "Now you can see, Herr SS-Reichsführer, where your procrastination has got you. Hitler will not reward you for your loyalty."

In a remarkable diatribe, Himmler apparently went on: "What's going to happen? It's all over, nothing can be saved now! I must take my life, I must take my life! Or what do you think I should do? Why don't you tell me? Tell me, tell me what I am supposed to do!"

Meanwhile, Hitler ordered Himmler's arrest and named Grand Admiral Karl Dönitz as his successor. After Hitler shot himself on April 30, Himmler met with Dönitz and offered his services as second-in-command, but Germany's new leader turned him down and formally stripped him of his posts. Kaltenbrunner took the opportunity to fire Schellenberg. Himmler went into hiding.

But Schellenberg did indeed travel to Sweden, although no longer to negotiate for Himmler's life. He arrived in the Swedish capital on May 5, four days after the news of Hitler's death was made public. Dönitz had sent him as an ambassador to offer the surrender of German troops in Norway. Treacherous Nazis had already done the same several days previously in Italy, where Anja's handler Guido Zimmer had been in the thick of it.

---

[47] Longerich, p.708.
[48] See Waller for a full account of Kersten's and Schellenberg's scheming.
[49] Waller, p.185-186
[50] See Wulff, Zodiac and the Swastika.

Secret Surrender

While Himmler was scrabbling around trying to salvage what he could of his reputation, his commanders on the ground shared the same concerns about what would happen to them when the conflict drew to an end. Many were directly implicated in war crimes and had similar ideas to Himmler about suing for peace. If only they could be the ones to bring peace to Europe, then perhaps they might be spared the hangman's noose. Some also had a more immediate reason for trying to end the war on their own terms, rather than be dragged into Hitler's death spiral — they were the men who would be forced to enact the Führer's scorched earth policy.

This was set to include the Fatherland itself, and Hitler confirmed as much to his architect Albert Speer, when questioned on the wisdom of destroying all public utilities, railways and bridges in Germany as the enemy approached.

"If the war is to be lost, the nation perishes," Hitler replied. "This is inevitable. There is no necessity to consider what the people would require for even a primitive existence. On the contrary, it is wiser to destroy these things ourselves. For this nation has been proved the weaker, and the future belongs solely to the stronger Eastern nations. Besides, those who remain after the battle are the inferior ones. The good ones have fallen."

Such a policy, even in the occupied territories, was a step too far for some Nazis, who realised that a fight to the finish would most likely result in their own needless deaths, as well as those of their men. And for the German commanders in Italy, defeat would also mean laying waste to the country's industrial northern heartlands and the cities of Milan, Genoa and Verona, shelling ports and other infrastructure, and destroying priceless cultural and historical artifacts. Before June 1944, when the Allies pushed the Germans further north, it would have meant obliterating Rome itself. Many of the top SS men in Italy had either developed an affinity for the country or had Italian ancestry themselves, and the recognition that they would be the ones responsible for wrecking the land that they loved was perhaps the final straw. Two men in particular, who for most of their careers had been loyal Nazis, found what they were being asked to plan beyond the pale.

SS-Obergrupenführer Karl Wolff was invariably described as tall, striking and handsome, and well-aware of his good looks. Blue-eyed and blonde, greying at the temples, he looked like an archetypal Nazi but insisted that he was also a good Catholic. Wolff had arrived in Italy on September 9, 1943, the day after the Armistice was made public. He had been dispatched to Italy alongside SS-Gruppenführer Wilhelm Harster, who was to be the Commander in Chief of the Security Police. Wolff was one of the most senior men in the SS hierarchy, level on rank with Kaltenbrunner. Only Himmler, with his title of SS-Reichsführer, was above them.

The Germans had created a position known as Higher SS and Police Leader to oversee police and military matters in occupied zones. But

Wolff, Himmler's former chief of staff and liaison officer between Hitler and Himmler, as well as between Himmler and Ribbentrop, the foreign minister, was far too important for even that grandiose title. Instead, a new position was created solely for him — Highest (Supreme) SS and Police Leader. It gave him complete authority over all German forces in Italy. Wolff later picked up another title, Plenipotentiary General of the Armed Forces for the Rear Combat Areas of Italy, giving him responsibility for rooting out partisans sowing chaos behind the Italian front.

Although Wolff had been awarded the Iron Cross for his service during World War One, he did not have a military or police background with the Nazis. Allen Dulles described him during his spell with Himmler as a "minister without portfolio", a diplomat who was able to manage the weird and not-at-all wonderful personalities of the Nazi hierarchy.[51] However, Wolff had made enemies of Kaltenbrunner and Schellenberg, who were both said to be jealous of his influence upon Himmler and Hitler. That being said, Wolff had also upset Himmler before his posting to Italy, by disobeying an order not to get divorced. Wolff had gone over Himmler's head and sought direct approval from Hitler. Himmler wanted the slippery Wolff out of the way, and Hitler trusted him immensely, so he became the perfect man to oversee the fraught situation in Italy.

Incidentally, Wolff had been great friends with, and a patient of, Felix Kersten, until he needed surgery for a kidney problem. He went under the knife of Kersten's great rival for Himmler's favour, Prof Karl Gebhardt, who told him that Kersten had massaged a stone into the kidney. Schellenberg believed this was untrue, and told him so, but it didn't stop Wolff hating Kersten from that moment on.

Despite his largely office-dwelling role, Wolff was already deeply implicated in the persecution of the Jews. He had ordered, in writing, the arrest of Jews in Frankfurt, and overseen deportations from the Warsaw Ghetto to Treblinka. In addition, standing alongside Himmler, Wolff had witnessed the shooting of Jews at Minsk in August 1941. In Italy, Wolff helped to organise the deportation of Jews and played a role in the Ardeatine Massacre. It's also worth recalling that Wolff was in overall command of forces that carried out numerous massacres and atrocities in Italy, including at Marzabotto between September 29-October 1, 1944, leaving 1,830 men, women, children and priests dead; at St Anna di Stazena in Luchesse, August 12, 1944, leaving 360 civilians dead; and at Vinca on August 24, 1944, where 108 partisans were shot dead.[52] His involvement in the subsequent peace talks does not absolve Wolff of these crimes.

The second key mover behind the Italian surrender plot was a man on Wolff's staff with whom he struck up an easy friendship. SS-Obersturmbanführer Eugen Dollman was a well-connected intellectual and aesthete who had lived in Italy since the late 1920s, when he moved there to study Renaissance history. Dollman joined the SS more by accident than design. In 1937, he visited Germany as an interpreter for a group of young Italian Fascists, who were to be given a personal reception by the Führer. When Hitler's own interpreter fell ill at the last moment, Dollman stepped in. Himmler, who was also at the event, was impressed and later hired Dollman as his interpreter during the holiday he took to Italy with Margerete.

From that point on, Dollman became the go-to guy for high Nazi officials visiting Italy, and for Italian officials going to Germany to see Hitler or Himmler. Dollman was eventually inducted into the SS, although he did not attend its training schools and served in the Nazi's Italian press office until he was appointed Ambassador to the Holy See in 1939. Like Wolff, Dollman had neither a police nor military background, but he served as Himmler's eyes and ears in Italy. What Himmler didn't know was that Dollman regarded him with a quiet contempt, and resented the war and the disruption it had brought to his happy life in Italy.

Allen Dulles described Dollman as "intellectual, highly sophisticated, somewhat snobbish and cynical". He very rarely wore the SS uniform, but Dollman stood out, with his slicked back, black hair, in an "Italian style" and "almost effeminate gestures".[53] Dulles may or may not have known that Dollman was secretly gay. Among the Germans officials with whom he became friendly was Kesselring, a fellow Italophile and another important figure in the surrender plot.

Shortly after his arrival in Italy, Wolff put the silver-tongued Nazi on his staff. Dollman was then able to introduce Wolff to all of his contacts at the Vatican, with whom Wolff had wanted to meet. In May 1944, this included an audience with the Pope, during which Wolff supposedly said he wanted to "commit his life to the cause of peace".

By then the military situation was deteriorating rapidly, with the Allies taking Rome on June 4 and Florence in early August, and then pushing on to just south of Bologna. The Germans were now boxed into the industrial northern heartland, with strongholds in the cities of Genoa, Milan and Turin. By the start of 1945, Kesselring was in sole control of the Italian front, and Wolff had based himself on the shore of Lake Garda, near Brescia, in the shadow of the Alps. The SS headquarters were in Verona, where Harster was stationed. Guido Zimmer's boss, Walter Rauff, oversaw the day-to-day activities in the area, which included combatting partisans. By early March 1945, the five Nazis — Wolff, Dollman, Harster, Rauff and Zimmer — were all part of a conspiracy to contact the Allies and convince Kesselring to surrender his forces.

By the time the treacherous quintet launched decisive action to bring the war in Italy to a close, Guido Zimmer, the corrupt and concupiscent spymaster, already faced problems of his own. In June 1944, the sadistic Gestapo prison boss Theodor Saeveke had moved into the ground floor of Zimmer's villa in Via Cimarosa, furnishing it entirely with items stolen from the apartment of an arrested partisan. Two more Gestapo men moved to the third floor in November 1944. It was an awkward situation — the corrupt foreign intelligence agent sandwiched between two units of violent secret policemen who would have had no qualms about liquidating him if they found out what he was up to.

Zimmer had to tread carefully. He was deeply implicated with the partisans and, according to now declassified files, he was already working as a double agent for the OSS, even before the surrender plot was launched.[54] Records show that there was fury within the organization after Zimmer failed to intervene when the Milanese Gestapo captured the leader of an OSS mission, Professor Pierre Ziccardi, codenamed Zucca, in Autumn 1944. Most galling to the Americans was the fact that Zucca was on his way to have a false identity card made for Zimmer and was in possession of his photograph, given to him by Zimmer, when he was detained. How the German got away with it was unclear. Zucca languished in San Vittore until the end of the war.

In January 1945, Zimmer wrote to his old housekeeper from Rome, Rosa Cappelli, asking her to work for him again. Zimmer wanted at least one person around the place he could trust. Rosa duly accepted and later became a font of information on Zimmer's personal life. She told the Americans how Zimmer seemed to lead a pleasant existence, entertaining many women and carrying on without a care in the world. She could recall the names of at least six mistresses, as well as another female visitor, who she believed to be an agent because she was careful about revealing her identity. This woman was aged about forty and described as "nervous" with a "tick in [her] eyes". She was said to speak German, and Italian with a southern accent. Given that Anja was not among the many names Rosa could recall visiting the villa, it's more than likely that the description of this colourful character refers to her. The question of whether Anja was simply one of Zimmer's spies or another of his many lovers remains open to interpretation.

In any case, Zimmer's post-occupational sabotage network, set up painstakingly and at great expense over several months, had to be scrapped after one agent was arrested. The Allies made the mistake of releasing this individual and allowing him to return to Switzerland, which afforded him the chance to warn Zimmer that the entire network was compromised. The agent provided a convincing level of detail, which had been imparted to him by his interrogators, and that was enough to persuade the German spymaster that all was lost. Zimmer began setting up a new network but it got no further than the planning stages, because in February 1945 Karl Wolff ordered him to begin looking for ways to open negotiations with the Allies in Switzerland.

It was well-known that the OSS had people in Switzerland — a wartime nest of spies, intriguers and ne'er-do-wells — who were open to hearing ideas for bringing the war to an end. Allen Dulles, the top man there and a future director of its successor organisation, the CIA, later wrote an extensive account of his experiences, publishing it as a book, *The Secret Surrender.*

Dulles had begun to receive "feelers" for peace in November 1944, not from the Western Front, as had been expected and hoped for, but from Italy. This came as a double surprise, because it was assumed that the Nazis would hold on tenaciously in Italy for a final redoubt in the Alps, and also because the feelers originated not from disgruntled professional military men of the Wehrmacht, but from the SS, whose members were mostly thought to be fanatics who would unquestioningly follow Hitler to the grave.

Dulles had always been skeptical of such approaches. In the past, German emissaries had offered not the unconditional surrender that the Allies had at Yalta agreed was the only path to peace, but rather a truce, with the aim of teaming up against the Russians. Often, such offers were viewed simply as a ploy to sow discord amongst the Allies, but in any case, the idea of making a deal was completely unacceptable — particularly as most of these approaches emanated from Himmler and Schellenberg, or alternatively Kaltenbrunner.

One such approach, to the British in Switzerland, came in Autumn, 1944. An Italian industrialist named Franco Marinotti claimed to be acting on behalf of Harster. Marinotti carried documentation from Harster assuring him that Himmler supported the efforts, and indeed Harster did write a report for Schellenberg. The offer was dismissed out of hand by the Allies. According to Dulles, a similar approach from an envoy of Schellenberg was made in February 1945, but Dulles refused even to see him. And again, at the end of the same month, an Austrian agent arrived from Vienna claiming to be there on behalf of both Kaltenbrunner and Himmler. The agent suggested that it might be possible to end the war by overthrowing Hitler's top leadership team, including Martin Bormann. It would, by implication, have meant liquidating the Führer himself. But there was a major sticking point —

nobody in their right mind would be willing to make a deal with the mass-murdering SS cult leader. It was something that Himmler consistently failed to understand.

At the same time, a more promising line emerged from the German Consul in Lugano, who let it be known that he had been sounding out German generals, including Kesselring, and SS figures Wolff and Harster, about the possibility of laying down arms. By the end of the month, these feelers appeared to be bearing fruit.

On February 25, 1945, Dulles and his assistant, the German economist Gero von Schulze Gaevernitz, had dinner by Lake Lucerne with Major Max Waibel from Swiss Military Intelligence. Waibel had been approached by an Italian industrialist, Baron Luigi Parilli, and his associate Max Husman, a Swiss professor known to Parilli through the tutelage of a relative. Parilli, of course, was an old business partner of Zimmer's — although at this point Dulles supposedly had never heard of Zimmer — and he claimed to be representing senior Nazi officials in Italy.

It was intriguing, but the neutral Swiss were unable to take on the negotiations themselves. They were keen to see a swift end to hostilities across the border, and while they no longer feared a German invasion, they didn't want to see the scorched earth policy enacted across North Italy, and nor did they wish to be burdened with tens of thousands of Italian refuges or, even worse, Nazis seeking asylum.

Gaevernitz went to meet Parilli and Husman the next day. Dulles later described Parilli as a "short, slight, bald gentleman with ingratiating manners...a bit like the keeper of a small Italian hotel who is trying to persuade you to take your dinner there". He was also a "rather talkative gentleman" and "a little pompous". Nevertheless, he appeared genuine.

Parilli seemed to be particularly exercised by a speech Mussolini had recently given in Milan, where he threatened "faithless Italians" with brutality at the hands of the Germans. Parilli wanted to end the war and become an "intervening angel" for North Italy. Parilli was pressed to explain how he could possibly bring such a thing about, and he began to elaborate on his friendship with Guido Zimmer, who he had first met when Zimmer was stationed in Genoa before his move to Milan. Parilli mentioned being a Knight of Malta, and he told Gaevernitz how Zimmer was also a devout Catholic. Zimmer was apparently "deeply troubled" by the prospect by enacting a scored earth policy, and wanted to save Italy's arts and religious treasures.

Parilli said that Zimmer had already broached the subject with Dollman, and said the higher SS man was receptive. In turn, Dollman had agreed to pass the idea to Wolff. Parilli said he did not know how Wolff had taken it, but he had applied for a visa and been waved through by the Germans, so somebody high up must be looking out for him, he reasoned. In reality, it was Wolff and Dollman who had recruited Zimmer, and Zimmer had recruited Parilli, although the Italian probably did not know this.

It was only much later that Zimmer's diaries would reveal how the spymaster had first offered up Parilli's name as a possible go-between back in November 1944, during a conference of SS leaders, including Wolff, in Verona. The plot was given the suggested codename Operation Wool. When Wolff gave the nod to begin in February 1945, Parilli, fearing the rise of Communism in the wake of a Russian conquest, had readily agreed. Zimmer immediately began making plans to acquire fake Italian passports and the rent of a villa in Turin, should he need to flee. Zimmer pointed out in his notes, with no hint of self-awareness, that more than one hundred Jews were already hiding out in the locale.

Parilli was chosen partly because he was close friends with Zimmer and the German felt he could trust him. But on the practical side, the noble (who Zimmer mostly referred to as "Baron X" in his diaries) had the advantage of having friends in very high places, both in Britain and America. He knew an Englishman named Ginnes, a personal friend of Churchill's then living in Switzerland; Lord Jones of Sheffield; and the MP Jack Robinson, married to the daughter of a friend of the Baroness Parilli. He also knew Howard A Lewis, a Jewish financier in America and adviser to Roosevelt.

Parilli initially planned to enter Switzerland and contact Ginnes, who could then get in touch with Robinson. At the same time, Parilli planned to telegram Lewis and attempt to entice him to Switzerland. As Zimmer wrote, "Baron X speaks English better than French; but in addition to

French, German and English, he masters a number of other languages. His huge wealth and his truly international family relations are going to stand him in good stead."

It was only after the negotiations had taken place, and Zimmer's shorthand notebooks were seized in Milan, that the Allies understood the long-standing relationship between the men, as one of "principal and agent". Zimmer called Parilli his "very sincere friend" and wrote, "I owe him greatest thanks for it was he who helped me to find the right way."

Gaevernitz was skeptical about the plan, given that Zimmer was really no more than a lowly functionary, but Waibel gave Parilli a password that would enable him to cross the border back into Switzerland with ease, if Wolff was serious. Nobody thought anything would come of it, least of all Dulles, who was more than happy to let Gaevernitz go off on a skiing trip. But just five days later, Waibel called Dulles. Parilli had shown up at the border with Dollman and Zimmer.

The Swiss intelligence man Waibel organised a meeting in the backroom of the Siaggi restaurant in Lugano. Present at this affair on March 3, 1945, were Parilli, Dollman and Zimmer, Professor Husmann, a Swiss intelligence officer named Fred Rothpletz, and an OSS agent named Paul Blum. Dulles had decided to keep the Germans at arm's length until he knew more. Wolff was also absent, but Dollman assured the party that he could convince the Supreme SS man in Italy to come to Switzerland. The discussions took place mostly in French, which Dollman translated into German for Zimmer. Blum later reported that there was "something hard in [Zimmer's] manner that indicates a possible police background". Dollman told the group he was officially representing Kesselring, Wolff and Harster.

Dulles wanted to make sure the Germans were serious, and through Blum asked them to free two partisan leaders who had been working with the OSS. Their names were the aforementioned Ferrucio Parri — who Anja had suggested she could seduce — and Antonio Usmiani. Parri was still being held in Verona, while the other fighter was kept in a Turin jail. Only Wolff would be able to free both high profile prisoners held in different parts of the country. Dollman agreed to do what he could.

Dulles and his men were highly skeptical, but they knew very little about Wolff and his resolve to surrender. Wolff himself later admitted that until early 1945 he had believed a compromise deal could be reached between Germany, Britain and America, because he had faith in Hitler's claims about a coming superweapon. However, after the failure of the Ardennes offensive and the realization that German forces had almost no air support, he became skeptical.

He had visited Hitler at his headquarters on February 6, 1945, ostensibly to take instructions for the scorched earth policy, but made a point of asking about new weapons. When it became apparent that no such weapons would be forthcoming, Wolff broached the subject of how to get out of the war. Hitler apparently did not say no to putting out feelers, and as Ribbentrop was in the room at the time, he too said he would look for a backchannel.

Two days later, Wolff relayed the details of the scorched earth program to his subordinates. He explained how it should work, but then told his commanders to carry out no acts of sabotage or destruction without his express permission. The meeting with Hitler had made up his mind — he was ready to act on the suggestion made by Zimmer a few months previously, and he would use Hitler's failure to say "no" as a get-out in case he fell foul of the leadership.

The biggest challenge for Wolff now that talks were underway was to bring the military onside, because without them there could be no meaningful surrender. Kesselring was a friend of the German ambassador to Italy, Rudolf Rahn, the most powerful Nazi civilian in the country, and both men badgered the old warhorse to join them, but initially he would only wish the men well with their "political plans".

Wolff also had to contend with spies in his camp. As soon as Parilli arrived back from the first trip to Switzerland, Wolff, Harster, Rauff and Zimmer convened at a small town near Lake Garda to discuss the next steps. One day after that meeting, Harster reported the details to Kaltenbrunner. Dulles later speculated that Harster might have done so with Wolff's permission, perhaps because both men wanted to hedge their bets against accusations of treachery. But given the fact that Harster was an ally of Kaltenbrunner's amid the factionalism of the RSHA, and that Wolff was an old confidante of Himmler's, it is more than likely he was acting alone to protect his own skin.

On March 8, 1945, a dramatic development took place. Much to Dulles' surprise, Parri and Usmiani were freed as requested. Not only that, but Zimmer personally drove them up to the Swiss border. Furthermore, Wolff also crossed into Switzerland, accompanied by Dollman, and his adjutant, all of course dressed in civilian clothes.

Wolff, Dulles later wrote, had "acted with astonishing speed". Dulles wondered how Wolff had accomplished everything in so short a time frame without worrying about cover stories or leaks. He pondered whether Himmler knew and approved of the meetings — which Wolff convincingly and accurately denied — and worried that Wolff was arrogant and reckless. In any case, it proved his commitment to the operation. As a result, the first encounter between Dulles and Wolff eventually took place in a ground floor apartment of a dingy building near Lake Zurich.

At this meeting, Wolff committed himself to an unconditional surrender, principally because it would be a crime against the German people to continue a futile conflict. "I control the SS forces in Italy," he told Dulles. "And I am willing to place myself and my entire organization at the disposal of the Allies to terminate hostilities." This was music to his ears, although Wolff pointed out that the military still needed to be brought onside. He vowed to try and bring Kesselring to Switzerland. Dulles excitedly relayed the details of the discussions to Allied Forces Headquarters at Caserta, and the plan was given an official codename — Operation Sunrise. It was now that things began to get dangerous.

The German contingent crossed back into Italy the next day, with Wolff vowing to speak to Kesselring. Rauff was waiting to meet him at the Italian Customs station, where he solemnly handed him a note — Kaltenbrunner wanted to see him in Innsbruck. The RSHA chief had been trying to reach him, with the result that Harster, who was now sidelined by Wolff, had once again wired to say that Italy's Supreme SS man was in Switzerland. Wolff put him off, explaining that he could not leave his post at this crucial juncture. But he knew it was only a matter of time until Himmler would want to confront him.

Through Parilli, Wolff asked the Allies to release a high-profile prisoner, to explain the purpose of his secret negotiations. He asked specifically for a favorite adjutant of Hitler's, Obersturmbannführer Wuensche. This ultimately proved to be impossible because Wuensche had been moved to a prisoner camp in Canada.

There was a secondary problem — Kesselring had also been summoned to the Führer's headquarters and was to be reassigned to the Western Front. The softening up work done by Rahn and Wolff seemed to have been in vain, and to make matters worse, after Wolff went to visit Kesselring in person, an Allied fighter plane shot up his car, injuring the chauffeur. Wolff asked if the Allied air forces could take it easy on cars travelling alone near Milan. Wolff once again gathered all his SS chiefs, including the questionable Harster, and told them in plain language that there was to be no violence of any kind against people or property, without his express permission

On March 19, Wolff, Zimmer, Wenner, Parilli, Waibel and Husmann again met OSS chiefs in Switzerland. This time, Wolff left Dollman behind at his headquarters to field any inquiries from Berlin, rather than trust the unreliable Harster. Allied Generals Lemnitzer and Airey also took part in the discussions, although they did not reveal their true identities.

It was at this meeting that Zimmer agreed to take on an extraordinary risk. Instead of continuing to use Parilli as a go-between, Dulles suggested installing an OSS wireless operator at his headquarters, so that communication could be near instantaneous. Before an agent could be found, Zimmer was forced to cross the border into Switzerland yet again. This time, on March 26, it was to inform the Allies that Wolf was having a hard time locating Kesselring. In fact, the situation was much worse than that.

On March 23, while visiting Kesselring's headquarters near Bad Nauheim, Wolff was ordered to Berlin. This time, he had no choice but to obey orders. He was driven by car, which was forced off the autobahn onto side roads several times by Allied planes, firing at anything that moved. In Berlin, he was whisked straight to the Reich Chancellery. It was 11.30am and the meeting took place in a small bungalow on the grounds occupied by Eva Braun's brother-in-law, Hermann Fegelein, who held Wolff's old job as liaison between Hitler and Himmler.

Himmler soon arrived, flanked by Kaltenbrunner. He immediately launched into an attack, telling Wolff that he knew of the meeting with Dulles and Gaevernitz on March 8. But rather than allege treachery, Himmler appeared more concerned with the fact that Wolff had not sought permission or the advice of his SD intelligence experts. Schellenberg, it appeared, was particularly aggrieved.

This line of attack gave Wolff some succour — he was not being accused of treason, but rather some sort of professional insult against Schellenberg. It became apparent to Wolff that Himmler still knew nothing of the subsequent meeting on March 19, which had involved the Allied 'military advisors' and was far more serious because the technical details of the proposed surrender had been discussed. In Wolff's mind, this narrowed the leak down to Harster, who he knew had told Kaltenbrunner of the first meeting. Wolff was convinced that Kaltenbrunner had engineered the order to come to Berlin so that he could scupper the surrender plans, clearing the path for him to pursue his own negotiations.

Wolff now decided to call their bluff. He suggested that all three of them should go to Hitler and tell the Führer how Wolff had established contact with the Allies with a view to capitulating in Italy. Himmler and Kaltenbrunner balked. They said it was a bad time and that Hitler was in a foul mood — it would only send him into a rage. Fine, Wolff said. With that the meeting was over. Himmler left, and Wolf and Kaltenbrunner endured an awkward lunch together at Kaltenbrunner's villa near the Wannsee.

Wolff discovered the next day that Harster had also been ordered to Germany for questioning and had been grilled by Amt VI specialists at a Bavarian castle doubling up as an evacuation centre. He didn't know much and so consequently had been able to tell them little. Kaltenbrunner drove Wolff to the castle, causing a bad crash on the way that flipped the car over. It was the second time that Wolff had nearly been killed in a motor incident in as many weeks, but neither he nor Kaltenbrunner were seriously injured. On the plus side, the entire episode convinced Wolff that Harster was clearly on his side, and not Kaltenbrunner's.

It was now March 26, and Wolff had still not been allowed to leave Germany. A meeting was held, chaired by Eugen Steimle, who was Schellenberg's Swiss-Italian specialist. Wolff managed to steer the conversion towards prisoner exchanges and peace feelers, rather than talk of surrender and treason, but Kaltenbrunner felt Wolff was being evasive. Closing the session, Kaltenbrunner told Wolff threateningly: "These contacts you think you have, we can get, any time, as well."

Both men returned to Berlin and Wolff was scheduled to see Himmler, but Hitler had ordered him to Hungary, so Wolff slinked off back to Italy. Himmler ordered Wolff not to visit Switzerland again.

Around the same time, Wolff moved his family south of the Brenner Pass, into the area under his control. On Easter Sunday, April 1, Himmler had them moved them back into Austria. He sent Wolff a chilling message: "This was imprudent of you, and I have taken the liberty of correcting the situation. Your wife and your children are now under my protection." Himmler warned Wolff not to leave Italy again. The implication was clear — Himmler could harm his family if the talks continued.

Badly spooked, Wolff failed to show in Switzerland for a scheduled meeting on April 2. Zimmer did turn up on April 4, followed by Parilli the next day. Wolff's ordure was relayed to Dulles and Gaeverntiz, but they were assured that he was over the jitters and would not back down in the face of Himmler's threat. He had since met with Kesselring's replacement General Vietinghoff on five occasions, gradually chipping away at his resolve to serve out his oath to Hitler. There was much back and forth as to how the surrender could be carried out while maintaining military honour, amid the question of whether or not German troops would have to surrender their arms or be detained. Vietinghoff was told that the Allies would discuss nothing but unconditional surrender. He came around to the idea only after receiving Kesselring's blessing.

In the meantime, Dulles organised the recruitment of a radio operator to embed himself at Zimmer's base in Milan. The man chosen was a twenty-six-year-old Czech named Vaclav Hradecky, a "short, stocky, black-haired, rather uncommunicative fellow" who Dulles nicknamed "Little Wally".

Wally had been arrested while studying in Prague in 1939 and sent to Dachau concentration camp. He was beaten, starved and generally mistreated by the SS for six months, before escaping. He lived underground in Germany for three years, secretly working for the Czech resistance. Wally was eventually caught and sent to a prisoner of war camp, but rather than admit he was an escaped concentration inmate, which would have meant certain death, he convinced his captors he was an escaped military prisoner. Wally escaped once again, made his way to Switzerland and then France, before making contact with the OSS.

Wally was brave, fearless, and completely unfazed when told that he would be turned over to an SS officer at the Swiss border and asked to carry out his work in the belly of the same beast that had tortured him for months at Dachau. Wally was to take Zimmer's messages and transmit them word for word, but was told no more about the ultimate purpose of the mission, and he asked no questions.

On April 13, Wally went along with Zimmer, taking with him his suitcase radio, code pads, signal plan, fresh underwear and socks, and an "enormous supply of cigarettes". At the start of the month, Zimmer had ordered Saeveke and his cronies to leave the villa in Via Cimarosa, so that Wally could be installed on the top floor. It must have raised suspicions but Zimmer, as ever, got away with it. The following day, the OSS agents were able to pick up his signal in Bern.

Shortly after this, an agent of Kaltenbrunner made another overture. This time, the RSHA boss sent Wilhelm Hoettl, a high-ranking and notorious SD man, who was coldly snubbed by Dulles. The Americans now had no need to speak with anyone else besides Wolff and his men. Soon, Zimmer was making his final trip to Switzerland behind the wheel of a dark blue Aprilia Bonecchi sports car. He had sent his chauffeur on holiday some days previously; apparently, he did not trust him.

There were several more twists and turns as the negotiations dragged on, including the fact that the Soviets became aware of the talks and wanted to take part. They were cleverly frozen out by the Americans. A further mini-crisis erupted when Allied headquarters almost gave up on the talks and ordered Dulles to have no more contact with the Germans.

The most serious threat was to Wolff's person from Himmler. On April 14, the SS-Reichsführer ordered him to Berlin once again. Wolff at first tried to put him off and wrote Himmler a letter, in which he claimed to be negotiating a truce against the Soviets. An incandescent Himmler repeatedly phoned his headquarters, but Wolff made sure he wasn't there to pick up the phone. Nevertheless, Wolff was put under increasing pressure to comply and eventually flew to Berlin on April 16. It was his turn, once again, to enter the belly of the beast.

Wolff later said that he had only agreed to go because he feared he would otherwise be replaced in Italy by a fanatical SS commander who would have no hesitation in carrying out the scorched earth policy. He put his chances of survival at about fifty-fifty. The journey itself was a perilous one — the plane flew at treetop level for most of the way to avoid Allied aircraft.

The next day, Wolff was driven to the Hohenlychen clinic. Himmler immediately launched into an attack, but Wolff produced a letter from Rahn, a favorite of Hitler, in which it was claimed that Wolff had achieved one of Hitler's objectives — namely holding up the Allied advance in Italy. It made Himmler think twice, and he appeared to calm down.

Later, Kaltenbrunner appeared, and took on the role of prosecuting advocate, laying out the evidence of Wolff's treason to the judge Himmler. Kaltenbrunner had with him a file of papers, but as Dulles put it: "Kaltenbrunner's bumbling agents had somehow never quite got the whole story straight." Wolff once again decided to call their bluff. He demanded to go to Berlin to see the Führer, accompanied by both of his accusers. Himmler demurred, claiming to be out of favour, but also probably fearful that his own parallel negotiations with Count Bernadotte might be known at the Führerbunker.

Wolff and Kaltenbrunner set off alone, spending the journey in stony silence lest the chauffeur be a spy. Just as they were about to enter the bunker at 3am Wolff abruptly stopped Kaltenbrunner in his tracks. He told the spy chief that if he denounced him in front of Hitler, or showed the Führer his secret reports, Wolff would tell Hitler that he had already informed Kaltenbrunner and Himmler of his activities back on March 24 and that it was they who had asked him not to tell their boss. It was one scorched earth policy that Wolff was prepared to see through. Wolff described Kaltenbrunner turning pale — some achievement since his face was normally always flushed red through drinking too much brandy.

Wolff was finally given an audience with the Führer at 4am. Kaltenbrunner and Feigelin were present, but remained silent. Hitler branded Wolff's approach to the Allies a "colossal disregard of authority" but did not go so far as to call it treason. Instead, he seemed more concerned that Wolff had acted without knowing the full extent of the Führer's plans. Wolff explained himself, placing great emphasis on the February 6 meeting with Hitler and Ribbentrop, at which the Führer had not said no to extending peace feelers. He discussed the March 8 meeting but nothing more. Wolff was convinced that Kaltenbrunner's spies knew next to nothing about the negotiations.

Hitler was cordial, but said he needed to sleep on it. By this point, the Nazi leader was a shadow of his former self. His right hand trembled, his features were sunken and his posture bent, his body flabby. At times, Wolff noticed, Hitler could barely stand and saliva dribbled from his mouth. Wolff was asked to return the next day, when the atmosphere in the bunker was feverish. Everyone except Hitler knew the war was lost, and many were privately scheming to make it out alive. One of them, Feigelin, would soon attempt to flee and would be shot for his troubles.

Hitler had no intention of leaving Berlin. He still believed that the Americans would turn on the Russians, and Hitler would use this turn of events to enter the "final battle". On which side? Wolff asked. "I will decide in favour of the side which offers me the most," Hitler replied. "Or the side which establishes contact with me first."

Wolff was instructed to hold steady, maintain contact with the Americans, but to get better terms — unconditional surrender was not an option. "Don't lose your nerve man," the desperate Führer told him. Kaltenbrunner's gambit to put Wolff out of the picture had failed. If anything, Wolff now had carte blanche to do as he pleased. Kaltenbrunner insisted on giving him one more order before he left: "Be sure no important civilian prisoners in your area fall into Allied hands. As the Allies approach, liquidate them."

When Wolff arrived back in Milan he immediately called for a bottle of champagne. He had charmed his way out of the death trap but was utterly exhausted. For a time, Wolff even seemed to waver in his resolve to continue the surrender talks, perhaps swayed by a resurgent feeling of loyalty to the semi-incapacitated Führer. On April 23, Himmler sent another message to Wolff, instructing him that, "No negotiations of any kind should be undertaken." But Wolff's response was unequivocal. "What Himmler has to say now makes no difference," he scoffed. Wolff was right, the war was quickly coming to its denouement.

Mussolini was captured and executed by Italian partisans on April 28. Hitler shot himself in his bunker on April 30, although the news did not get out until May 1. But by then, on April 29, with most of the main parties at Allied headquarters in Caserta, the surrender of the German forces in Italy was signed, and it went into effect at noon on May 2.

Exactly how many lives were saved is impossible to know, coming as it did only one week before Germany's general surrender on May 8. But it certainly would have spared hundreds at least, not including those who would otherwise have been killed during the long weeks of negotiations, when Wolff had ordered his SS men to refrain from violence.

***

The question remains as to what role Anja might have played in the schemes of both Himmler and Wolff. There is no doubt that Himmler desperately wanted Anja to go to Switzerland. On the face of it, the well-connected Finn would have been the right sort of person to extend peace feelers to the British, among whom Anja had plenty of contacts. There was really no other reason for Himmler to send an agent to Switzerland by that point in the war — and considering the efforts he and Schellenberg made to instigate a successful mission of this nature, it seems the most logical conclusion.

However, the passage in Wilfred Wulff's book offers an alternative context. Perhaps Himmler merely wanted to ensure that Anja stayed alive long enough to offer him a place to hide out should the worst happen. This explanation solves the question as to why he was apparently happy to pay her medical bills. She was, after all, top of his mind when the crisis sparked by the Reuters report erupted on April 28.

On a similar note, Anja's former handler Klaus Hügel believed that Himmler wanted to flee to Switzerland, and that Anja was to act as some sort of advance agent of influence who could convince the Swiss that he was not such a bad guy. But when Himmler was going through his options with Wulff and Schellenberg, he made no mention of going to Switzerland, only of Anja's non-existent estates in Finland and Lapland.

In the meantime, Anja was still living in Milan when Wolff put his surrender plans into action. They would not have been possible without Guido Zimmer, Anja's handler and, quite plausibly, her lover. How much of Zimmer's activity would she have been aware of? And it is possible that she was able to feed information back to Himmler, resulting in Wolff's two dangerous trips to Germany?

We know that Kaltenbrunner, not exactly a great friend of Himmler or Schellenberg, knew about Wolff's plotting, but Dulles thought that to be the result of Wilhelm Harster covering his own back. Also, according to Schellenberg, Kaltenbrunner generally showed little interest in foreign intelligence matters, and therefore it's unlikely that he would usually have dealt with minor agents such as Anja.[55] However, it's certain that Kaltenbrunner knew who Anja was because he had been present at the meeting with Schellenberg and Harster in Thuringia, after which Harster write a report recommending she be removed from Italy. It would explain how Kaltenbrunner's "bumbling agents" never quite knew the full extent of Wolff's plotting.

Schellenberg, as Himmler's 'plenipotentiary,' probably knew Anja better and might have established a way to communicate with her that bypassed Zimmer and Kaltenbrunner. In his extensive post-war debrief and memoirs, Schellenberg was neither asked about, nor proffered any information, in regards to Anja Manfredi. This perhaps underlines the fact that although she was connected in very high places, Anja was a very low level agent. In fact, Schellenberg seemed to know very little about the SD's work in Italy towards the end of the war, and stated that counter-espionage activities there were still in their early stages. Schellenberg's efforts had mostly been focused towards extending peace feelers to elements in Switzerland and Sweden. Yet on this matter Anja might have been an invaluable resource.

As a relatively inexperienced and not-particularly discreet spy, Anja would probably have been able to pass on patchy information letting Himmler know that something was afoot, without really knowing all the details. Of course, this is speculation and there is no written account that suggests Anja knew anything about Zimmer's plotting nor that she passed on information to Kaltenbrunner, Schellenberg or Himmler. However, it would explain why Himmler seemed to know that Wolff was continuing the talks with the Americans even though Kaltenbrunner's information was limited. As we know, Anja was still on his mind as the regime crumbled, suggesting he had recently been in contact with her and knew where she was.

Speaking to his British interrogators at Camp 020 in early August 1945, Klaus Hügel suspected that Anja had foreseen the Nazi defeat and became less keen on going to Switzerland. He thought she most probably made "other arrangements for her security" as the Allies closed in.

Hügel also offered several ideas about what had happened to Anja since the fighting ended. Either she was dead; had escaped the clutches of the Italian Resistance by pretending to be loyal to them, despite her association with Himmler; she had been arrested in Italy; or that she had joined the German retreat in Milan to South Tyrol. In fact, on July 20, 1945, Anja was under observation by US forces in Rome, prompting the request to Camp 20 for Hügel to be interviewed.

Anja was deemed to be "highly strung" and the Americans wanted to know whether or not they should bring her in for questioning.

Eventually, in September 1945, Anja was arrested by US forces and later transferred to a British prisoner camp, until her release in March 1946. If the records of her time there have survived they are not publicly available. A Freedom of Information request to the CIA only elicited the response that staff could "neither confirm nor deny" their existence. Instead, the agency would only point to the files of Zimmer and Hildegaard Beetz, a German journalist and SD agent in Rome who had dealings with Kaltenbrunner, and who later provided the Allies with a list of German operatives in Italy. Anja's name was among them.

Anja certainly did have a file at one point — two in fact — whose references appear among Zimmer's files. They were referred to as "JZX-4032. 9/10/45, MANFREDI DE BLASIIS, Baroness Anja, X-2, Rome" and "CIC, RAAC, Case No. R-2347 of 5 Sept 1945". The former suggests that Anja was interviewed by the X-2 branch, the special OSS unit specializing in counter espionage and running double agents. Given that there is no firm evidence that Anja was a double agent it's possible that she was assessed for her suitability as a post-war operative. Then again, she might merely have been questioned about other personalities who she'd encountered in Italy.

It is certain that Anja would have been asked about her relationship with Himmler and his secret plans, but exactly what she said, like so much of her story, remains a mystery. However, Anja did discuss her time in wartime Italy more than a decade later, when she claimed to be owed compensation for persecution by the Nazis. It was, perhaps, her most audacious scheme yet.

---

51 Dulles, Ibid.
52 Lamb, p.68.
53 Dulles, p.47-49.
54 See Zimmer files.
55 Schellenberg files, UK National Archives.

The Baroness

Final Gambit

Heinrich Himmler took the coward's way out by biting down on a cyanide capsule on May 23, 1945, two days after his capture while disguised, poorly, as a Sergeant Heinrich Hitzinger. He had made it only as far as Bremervorde, near Bremen, some two hours from Lübeck. His body was buried in an unmarked grave in Lüneberg, close to the British camp where he met his ignominious end.

Himmler's first mistress, Hedwig Potthast, had last visited him at the SS clinic on March 22, two days after Hitler stripped him of his military responsibilities. She spoke to him by phone for the final time on April 19, when he signed off with the "hope that God would protect her, the children, and Germany". But, Himmler had told her, things were "more difficult every day".

Himmler had phoned Margarete around the same time, and on April 20 — Hitler's birthday — she packed up her belongings, their daughter Gudrun, her sister Lydia and other female relatives, and took a car bound for the South Tyrol. Hedwig also made a break for the same border as the Allies closed in on Berchtesgaden, where bombing eventually badly damaged the cottage.

Allied troops later found Margarete and Gudrun hiding out in the Tyrol on May 13, 1945. They were taken to a British interrogation camp near Rome, via Verona and Florence. When Himmler's dutiful but long-suffering wife was later told of his death by an American journalist, she expressed no emotion, preferring not to give reporters the satisfaction. On the question of the death camps, she pleaded ignorance and said she was "just a woman" who "did not understand politics".[56] She had opted not to take her own cyanide capsule, which was later found sewn into the shoulder padding of her coat.

Mother and daughter were both interrogated, and Margerete was confronted with the spectre of her husband's second 'wife', Hedwig. She pretended not to even know her name and merely conceded that she knew Himmler had been unfaithful. Hedwig, who had also been captured in Austria, was interrogated on May 22, 1945, and described Himmler as "an idealist with tremendous faith in Germany and in the Führer". The interrogator remarked that Hedwig was "attractive" and an "unassuming woman rather than a forceful or calculating one".[57] Neither woman was asked about Anja Manfredi.

Hedwig was released and later tried to erase her past, insisting that she knew nothing of Himmler's activities during the war nor of the human furniture in her Berchtesgaden attic. Margerete and Gudrun were kept in camp until November 1946 and Himmler's wife later faced several trials and appeals, where she was variously categorized as a Lesser Offender or Follower (both to huge public protests) and then Offender, resulting in the loss of property and money linked to Himmler, as well as her voting rights. Gudrun became a vocal defender of her father and worked tirelessly for the post-war Nazi organisation Silent Help, as well as other neo-Nazi groups. Margerete died in August 1967, at the age of 74, while Hedwig lived until 1994, when she died at the age of 82.

Some of the old Nazis in Anja's life probably used Gudrun's services — many of them certainly thrived. Her former handler Klaus Hügel went to work as a corporate lawyer for the motor company Porsche, whose founder, Ferdinand Porsche, was himself an SS member who had supplied vehicles for the Nazi cause, including the V-1 flying bomb. But in 1951, the year that Porshe died, Hügel was suspected of continuing involvement in espionage. The CIA believed he was a courier carrying secret documents to Vienna for the Soviets.[58] Observations continued until he was detained and questioned in 1962.

Hügel denied having dealings with any intelligence services after his release from Allied custody in 1947, but declassified files show that he did receive visits from numerous SD figures, including Himmler's old lackey Eugen Steimle, who he saw in 1959 or 1960, and again in 1961. Other sources claimed he had associated with Karl Wolff, Otto Skorzeny, the man who led the mission to free Mussolini, and ex-Gestapo man and expert on the Rote Kapelle, Heinz Pannwitz. The Americans were certain that Steimle was working for Uphill, the codename for the West German Foreign Intelligence Service (BND), and they thought it fair "to assume" that Hügel was likewise employed.

Immediately after the war, the OSS recruited Guido Zimmer to work as an agent once again, this time by penetrating the fanatical Freikorps Adolf Hitler, then thought to have some 16,000 members hellbent on resurrecting the Third Reich. Zimmer had re-emerged in Milan in August 1945, wearing an American uniform and telling Allied forces that he intended to go to North Africa, from where he would write a report on Germans returning from the Russian-occupied zone. He was taken up on the offer, but there is no record of the result.

In February 1946, Zimmer asked for American protection so that he could return to Rome with his wife Kathie, and children Klaus Luigi and Luisa. The children were said to be "desperately ill of tuberculosis" but the Americans were either unwilling or unable to help. The Italians wanted Zimmer to be treated the same as other SS figures, despite his leading role in Operation Sunrise. (Karl Wolf, for example, was jailed for four years in 1948 and then sentenced to another fifteen years in 1968, for deporting 300,000 Italian Jews to Treblinka. He was released in 1971 after suffering a heart attack).

Although the dominant American view was that Zimmer's role in Sunrise was overstated and that he was in fact an "incompetent" spy, Allen Dulles called him the "most important liaison officer" with his counterpart Wolff, pointing out that "without Zimmer's help, at the risk of his life, the surrender negotiations would have been exceedingly difficult, if not impossible". After all, he had sheltered the OSS radio operator Wally in Milan. But Dulles couldn't convince the Italians and all contact with Zimmer apparently ceased. He later became Baron Parilli's private secretary for matters pertaining to the Knights of Malta. Zimmer was also seen associating in SS circles as late as 1950.

Meanwhile, Herbert Kappler was jailed for life in 1948. He developed terminal cancer and escaped from prison hidden in a suitcase carried by his wife in 1977, dying at home in Germany six months later. Freidrich Engel, also known as the Butcher of Genoa, escaped punishment for most of his life, but was convicted of the murder of fifty nine Italian prisoners in a Hamburg court in 2002. His sentence was suspended because of his age, and the conviction later overturned. Wilhelm Harster, implicated in the murder of more than 100,000 Jews, was sentenced to twelve years in prison in 1948, for his role in the deportation and murder of thousands of Dutch Jews. He was released after just four years and became a civil servant in Bavaria. In 1967, he was sentenced to a further fifteen years, but was pardoned in 1969. Eugen Dollman hid out in a Vatican-run mental institution after the war and the CIA later helped him to settle in Switzerland under a false identity. After that, he worked for Otto Skorzeny in the arms trade and then continued to work as a translator. Ernst Kaltenbrunner was found guilty of crimes against humanity at the Nuremburg trials and hanged in October 1946. Walter Schellenberg gave evidence at the trial, but was himself sentenced to six years in prison for his role in the murder of Soviet POWs. He was released after two years because of ill health, and died from a liver condition at home in Turin in 1952.

Anja's long-suffering first husband Hans Götz found himself in much more elevated company. At the end of the war, Hans returned not to Hamburg, his family's home for generations, but to Copenhagen, the city that had taken him in when his fellow countrymen hounded him and his family out of Germany. He was soon appointed head of the antiquarian division of the publishing house Branner, returning to one of his specialisms — creating catalogs, including in 1949 one to celebrate the

200th anniversary of Goethe's birth. Hans became a shareholder in the company, and by 1952 had become the majority owner. Three years later he began the process of claiming reparations from Germany.

The system was bogged down in bureaucracy. Firstly, Hans no longer had the paperwork to prove his income from the business in Hamburg. It took the intervention of fellow booksellers Ernst Hauswedell and Max Bahr to convince the authorities of the bookstore's significance.[59] Finally, in 1958, Hans was awarded a lump-sum compensation amounting to DM 12,690 for damage to professional advancement. Compensation for his forced flight to Sweden from the Danish capital was refused in 1960, because the 'damage' did not occur within the territory of the Reich.

Separately, Hans was enraged when Danish colleagues in the publishing world tried to keep him out of the national and international antiquarians' association because he had allegedly maintained contact with German antiquarians during the war. In their view, Hans was a collaborator. It was not until 1956 that Hans won back his Danish association membership in court.

The high point of his career in Denmark was the auction of the collection of the engineer Oscar Ekman and his wife Lia Ekman, which took place in 1965. It was considered to be one of the most comprehensive Danish book auctions of the twentieth century and Hans personally edited the elaborately produced catalog. The following year, in April 1966, he died in Copenhagen.

Hans did eventually return to Hamburg, but only to be buried. His daughter, by then named Maria Bloch, continued to run the business in Copenhagen until 1996. Hans died without knowing something that would have infuriated him even more than the behaviour of the obstinate Danish booksellers — his ex-wife Anja had launched her own bid for compensation. The woman who had bankrupted him, spied for Himmler, and then failed to speak up for his mother, aunt and cousin as they suffered in the ghetto, was now claiming to be a victim of the Nazi regime.

***

Baroness Anja Manfredi de Blasiis spent her immediate post-war years fighting off Filippo's attempts to divorce her. Following her release from Allied custody, she continued to live in Rome, spent time in Switzerland apparently working as a press agency stringer, and frequently travelled to Germany for medical treatment.

Unsurprisingly, Baron Manfredi was not keen to reconcile with his wife. He held her fully accountable for his kidnap and imprisonment by the British, even though it was his deal with Koehler that had landed him in hot water. The divorce case took until October 10, 1952, to come before Rome's ecclesiastical court, or Tribunale del Vicariato, where the marriage was declared "null and void" because Anja's previous marriage with Hans had produced a child, and so was considered to be extant. Anja appealed for re-instatement of the marriage, and successfully had the decision overturned six years later on December 20, 1958, a process that her lawyer described as taking "an unusually long time".[60] By then, the Baron had already remarried, in 1955, to a daughter of the engineer Oscar Sismondo. They remained happily married until his death in the early 1990s.

With her finances more stretched than ever, Anja chose to open up another legal campaign. Nearly fourteen years after the end of World War Two, and aged nearly sixty, she wrote to the German embassy in Rome to enquire about making a claim for reparations over her arrest in 1944, and she followed that up in March 1959 with a formal application to the State Office for Reparations.

At the time of the application, Anja's victory in the divorce case was still to be confirmed, meaning that she had not been "reinstated in her full civil rights as the wife of Baron Manfredi". As her Freiburg-based lawyer, Walter Scheffel, explained, this was crucial because since the divorce, "She had lost these rights [and] Baron Manfredi was no longer obliged to look after my client and did not pay any more".[61]

Scheffel set out in writing a summary of his client's history, including her marriage to Hans Götz, the birth of her son, and subsequent marriage to Baron Manfredi. It did not take much reading between the lines to understand why Anja was now applying for reparations. Nevertheless, Scheffel spelt it out:

> My client has found herself in dire straits that cannot be described. Nor would she be able to resolve this emergency through her own work, because she is not able to work regularly as a result of permanent serious illnesses. My client hoped to receive her rights as Baroness Manfredi much sooner; the proceedings before the church courts have been dragging on for over six years, as I can confirm from my own knowledge. Only when the impression arose that there was no end to the proceedings in sight did my client turn to the German embassy in Rome in May 1958 to apply for compensation.

Scheffel followed this explanation with a description of Anja's arrest in Genoa, which she said took place on April 30, 1944. But this account bore little resemblance to the one given by Klaus Hügel at Camp 020 in 1945.

Anja now claimed that her arrest was "carried out by the SD, I assume that it was an agency of the SiPo and the SD in Genoa". Scheffel added that, "A Sturmbannführer Engle (sic) in Genoa and an SS member named Zimmer were involved. My client does not know their whereabouts." Both men, of course, had been involved in handling Anja for the SD, whereas according to Hügel, it was the Abwehr that had ordered her arrest and the SD was only involved because it was in the process of absorbing the military intelligence agency.

In any case, Scheffel said Anja was subsequently transferred from Genoa to Verona, and sentenced to death by a court martial:

> The conviction was not based on any legal basis. My client was not accused of any crimes of the common law. The arrest and conviction obviously took place for political reasons. First of all, my client was first married to a Jew, which made her suspicious to the Nazis from the outset.

Scheffel went on to note that the divorce from Hans had taken place in 1928, not for "racial reasons," but because the couple had simply grown apart. At the time, he said, Anja had been Protestant and later converted to Catholicism. But he suggested that Anja's subsequent marriage to Baron Manfredi, and the couple's antipathy towards the German occupiers, had also played a part:

> She is very intelligent and interested in politics. Their opposing attitude towards Nazism did not go unnoticed. There is absolutely no explanation for her arrest and her sentencing to death other than that she should be eliminated as a dangerous opponent of Nazism. For a better understanding it should be noted that my client's uncle was the Finnish ambassador in Rome. The Baron Manfredi is wealthy, and therefore influential. My client was therefore not viewed as an insignificant person.

Scheffel said that after spending "some time waiting for the execution of the death sentence," Anja was taken to Berlin in September 1944. "It is unlikely that it will be possible to clarify why this happened," he wrote. "The Reich Security Main Office presumably believed that it could obtain valuable information from my client. My client was freed as a result of the war and immediately returned to Italy. She was arrested there in September 1945 by the Americans, was transferred to the British and was only released by them in May 1946."

There is no doubt that Hügel's account of Anja's wartime activities is far more reliable than her version. Not only did Hügel have nothing to lose by telling his captors the truth, his statement was extremely detailed and vivid. Some elements were also backed up by Baron Manfredi, in particular the meeting with Himmler, which Anja did not mention in her version of events.

Her timeline was also directly contradicted by entries in Rauff's and Zimmer's OSS files, particularly Zimmer's, because contained within those papers there are highly incriminating snippets from Anja's interrogation by the Americans. For example, although we do not have her complete account, Anja told her captors that Hügel had asked her to go to Florence in May 1944 to spread Nazi propaganda, and later that summer to do the same thing in Switzerland. Anja said she refused on both occasions. But while seeking reparations, she claimed that she had been in imprisoned during this period.

Another snippet shows that Anja's OSS interrogators found her to be highly unreliable. As their report dated September 10, 1945, stated:

> It is the opinion of these agents that Subject's friendship with Himmler and her many appeals to him for help absolutely controvert her denial that she ever received money or missions from the SS or SD. Nor can she be heard to pass off lightly her dealings with such notorious SS and SD officials such as Col. Dollman, Kapler, Engel, Zimmer and Huegel. She claimed only to have seen them a few times and then merely to ask personal favours of them.

Anja's claim to have been taken to Berlin against her will is the most blatant lie of all. Klaus Hügel described how, after Himmler intervened to free her from custody, Anja went to the German capital on a voluntary basis in July or August 1944, and then took a second trip, where she boasted of seeing Himmler, in October or November. That Christmas, Himmler and Anja exchanged gifts. Beyond that, there are numerous written records showing her presence in Milan throughout 1944 and 1945. Hügel also described a negative report written about Anja by Harster, before Hügel saw her for the last time, in Italy, on February 16, 1945. Anja certainly had not spent these months in custody in Berlin.

If Anja had provided any level of detail about her questioning, stated reason for arrest, or even exactly where she was supposedly held in Berlin, it might be possible to give her some benefit of the doubt. But there was no elaboration.

Instead, Anja was only interested in pointing out, through her lawyer, how the spell in captivity had made her unwell. Anja claimed that it was after April 30, 1944, the supposed date of her arrest, that she contracted stomach tuberculosis. As a result, between 1945 and 1946 she underwent three operations, and by the time of the application she had been through a further twenty-two procedures, which Scheffel said "seems credible to me because I know from my own knowledge that my client has repeatedly had to undergo such operations in Freiburg".

Whether or not Anja really had twenty-five operations between 1945 and 1959 is open to question — it sounds remarkably high. But it also throws into doubt her entire medical history, right back to her days with Hans Götz and the alimony payments that left him bankrupt.

Anja had supposedly been seriously ill since at least 1934, when she moved to Rome. Already by 1944, as far as Baron Manfredi was aware, she had undergone at least fifteen operations. Anja did not mention these in her application. The Americans, in one of their reports, suggested that Anja was a "neurasthenic" — essentially someone suffering with a poorly defined chronic fatigue condition. Anja must have gone under the knife at some point, because bills were certainly paid. But was Anja, like Himmler, something of a hypochondriac? Did she exaggerate a genuine condition as a means to generate income? Her frequent bouts of illness certainly gave her a reason to travel and to borrow large sums of money.

Anja's application was accompanied by a letter in support from a Dr B Müller, Freiburg, dated February 17, 1958. The doctor faithfully relayed the same story of Anja's arrest and imprisonment, although he said it only lasted from April 30 to June 1944, more in line with the account given by Hügel and a sloppy oversight on her lawyer's part. He also said the diagnosis of intestinal tuberculosis was made in 1947, and that she had undergone several operations both before and after coming into his care in 1952. "Her health has deteriorated steadily due to poor diet, completely inadequate living space and care, as well as attempts to earn a living and cover the high costs of the procedures," he wrote. "Several times I was forced to admit the patient to the hospital in a life-threatening condition." The doctor went on:

The complaints have now worsened. The patient is usually bedridden and unable to do even light work. The first and most important cause of the severe intestinal suffering could have been the SD imprisonment and the sentencing to death and the associated agonizing expectation of execution. The sudden change in the environment, combined with the inferior nutrition and emotional shocks, brought about the complete shattering of the physical resistance of the patient, who had been living in the best of circumstances until then. In my opinion, these burdens led to the development of intestinal tuberculosis in 1944, which made three abdominal operations necessary. A causal link between the health damage suffered in captivity and the current incapacity for work can be assumed.

Anja gave her address as Via della Colonna Antonina 52, Rome, and her occupation as pressanalytikerin, or press analyst. She indicated on the form that her application was being made because of persecution due to political opposition to Nazism and for reasons of faith.

But she also admitted to having lived in Switzerland on December 31, 1952, which caused the authorities to ask the Swiss police for her details. Perhaps unsurprisingly, given her history, Anja had failed to register there. It was a red flag. It also began an interminable exchange of letters between Anja's lawyer and the authorities over which reparations office, Freiburg or Karlsruhe, should process the application. Scheffel was insistent that the matter should be handled in Freiburg, because that was Anja's "second home" if not in Rome. It meant that both he and the administrative clerk could speak to Anja personally if required. Scheffel also took the opportunity to explain more about Anja's whereabouts and occupation post-war.

Anja had found work with an American press agency in Heidelburg, Germany in 1950, he said, but she had also lived and worked in Switzerland and Rome while dealing with the divorce proceedings. She returned to live in Freiburg permanently in the spring of 1953, apparently at the instigation of the then-Archbishop of Freiburg, Dr Wendelin Rauch, an outspoken critic of the Nazis. In Freiburg, Anja lived with a Mrs Scholl, Erwinstr 28, and then with lecturer Kurt Holmberg, at Handelstr 24. By this point, she had left the employ of the Americans and was working for a French agency.

Anja then embarked on a bizarre and short-lived new career. From the spring of 1954 to October 1954, she was employed by a shipping line. This must have been aboard the TSS Olympia, owned by the Greek Line, because a passenger manifest for May 5, 1954, shows an Italian woman named Anja Manfredi arriving in New York from Bremerhaven, a German port not far from Hamburg. She was listed among the ship's crew as a "social hostess" and had been engaged by the company that March in Cherbourg. She arrived again in New York on May 31. This work seems rather out of character, and life on the high seas must not have suited her, because Anja moved back to Freiburg until October 1956, and then returned to Rome to continue fighting the divorce, until the time of the reparation application.

Anja's excuse for not registering with the Swiss police was that she was working for the American agency, and they had told her it was unnecessary. "My client is a generous person who pays no special attention to such formalities and therefore did not feel compelled to double-check whether the Americans had given her accurate information," Scheffel wrote. Anja had also failed to register in Freiburg, he accepted, but she did so when the police contacted her.

Scheffel insisted that even though she was a naturalised Italian, Anja wanted to settle in Germany, as she had done during her eleven-year marriage to Hans. He said her split from the Baron had "made her feel German again" and that after the war she "would have stayed in Germany forever if she had not succeeded in having the ecclesiastical court establish the nullity of her marriage". He added: "She speaks and writes German like her mother tongue."

The reparations agency duly made inquiries in Hamburg; with the Americans; and with the German embassy in Rome, noting that: "It is hardly unreasonable to trace back the previous persecution of the applicant, who appeared to be suspected of espionage." For this reason, they asked Scheffel to find out more about why Anja had been arrested by the Germans, as well as subsequently by the Americans. The agency also took steps to lower Anja's expectations, pointing out that because she was an Italian citizen until at least 1947, she was governed by the Italian peace treaty of that year which had waived all claims against Germany. Meanwhile, the US mission in Berlin responded to say it held no files on Anja Manfredi.

Scheffel's reply was vague and evasive. He suggested the names of three people who might be able to explain the reasons for her arrest: Baron von Hackwitz, from the German Embassy in Rome; Prince Dimitri Galitzina, Bordighera, Villa la Cava; and Professor Attorine Baldussi, Genoa. He also returned a signed affidavit by Anja, made at the Rome embassy in December 1962, and witnessed by von Hackwitz. This is the only known written account by Anja of her wartime activities. While it lacks any real detail, it is worth recounting in full:

> In April 1944, I was staying at the Hotel Colombo in Genoa. There I was arrested on April 30, 1944 by Italian carabinieri on behalf of the SD and immediately brought to Verona. In Verona, because of my health, I was admitted to the prison ward of the Ospedale Civile, where I was under constant surveillance. After the hospital near the train station was bombed, I had an operation in a village near Verona. I don't remember the name of the village exactly. After I was able to travel again I was first transported to Innsbruck in an SD motor vehicle and from there by train to Berlin. That happened in September 1944. The reason for my arrest was given to me that I had spied against Germany in cooperation with Count Folke Bernadotte. I assume, however, that the fact that I was married to a Jew in the first place also played a role in my arrest.

There was no elaboration on what had supposedly happened to her in Berlin, no mention of a court martial or death sentence, and no explanation of how, when or why she was released. Furthermore, she made no attempt to discuss her arrest by the Allies after the war. Anja did add:

> I do not have any documentary evidence for the duration of my term of detention and am therefore in need of evidence. I have been instructed that knowingly or negligently submitting a false affidavit is a punishable offence and, in lieu of an oath, I affirm that I am not aware of anything that contradicts the correctness of my above information. This affidavit is to be presented to the state office for reparation in Karlsruhe. I therefore ask for a fee exemption.

Anja's problem was that she had absolutely no way of knowing what others had committed to paper about her. It's telling that she waited for more than a decade before coming forward. Bernadotte was no longer around to ask — he had been assassinated by the Stern Gang in Israel in 1948. There is no indication that Anja even knew Bernadotte, nor that he would have been suspected of spying against Germany back in the summer of 1944. It was a gamble, but she must have felt the odds of being found out had shortened dramatically in her favour after such a long time. But would it pay off? The decision was handed back to Anja's lawyers on January 23, 1963:

> Due to damage to freedom and body or health, the state office for reparations in Karlsruhe has decided: 1/The application is rejected. 2/The decision is made free of charge; fees and expenses are not reimbursed.

It must have come as a crushing blow. This had been Anja's last roll of the dice. In a long report, the agency set out its reasons. In its view, there was no evidence that Anja had been arrested or imprisoned for her opposition to Nazism. Anja's claim that there could be no other reason could only be treated with "the utmost reservation". The authors also noted the fact that she had decided not to repeat the claim about a death sentence in her legally binding affidavit. The agency suggested Anja had merely been arrested for espionage, and whether the charge was accurate or not, it was not a politically-motivated act:

> It appears credible that the applicant was arrested on suspicion of espionage. Such an assumption is justified by the fact that Italy joined the Allies after the surrender in September 1943 and that the area that the German troops still owned from Italy was under German occupation. It is understandable that the Italians opposed the occupation regime with all their might — insofar as they were not Fascists. In times like these, it is easy to be suspected of espionage, especially if you belong to a leading social class with international connections.

The agency made a further observation casting doubt on the claim that her arrest had been politically motivated — Anja was not sent to a concentration camp, as had happened to almost all other political prisoners of the Nazi regime. The fact that she was later interned by the Americans and the British was further grounds for suspicion of espionage:

This offence is not only punishable according to Nazism, but is treated with the most severe punishments in every state in the world, including in western democracies. During the war, proven espionage was almost always punishable by death.

In fact, there was no strong evidence that Anja would have been deemed a political opponent of Nazism, because not only was she an Italian, she had displayed no clear antipathy towards the regime. Furthermore:

The applicant's assumption that her first marriage to a Jew played a role in the arrest could not be accepted. Such a reason for arrest is unlikely. This marriage was divorced in 1928, long before the so-called 'seizure of power'. So far, the compensation authority has not become aware of any case that such an earlier dissolved marriage had ever brought disadvantages to an Aryan spouse, even in Germany during the Nazi regime. In addition, it seems extremely questionable whether the German authorities knew about it before the applicant was arrested, especially since the applicant had remarried. It may well be that the interrogating officers pointed to this point in the course of the interrogation and then exploited it. However, the conclusion that the applicant has been arrested for this cannot be drawn. The application therefore had to be rejected.

Anja was sixty-three years old, alone, unemployed, and ostensibly sick. Her last shot at a major pay day, riddled with holes as it was, had fallen through.

***

And there our story about Baroness Anja Bergroth Manfredi de Blasiis abruptly ends. She died on December 28, 1975, taking her secrets to the grave. Although she did keep up a correspondence with her sister Judith right up until the end, Anja left behind no known account of her wartime activities, bar the brief and demonstrably false claims she made in her application for reparations. Examples of her journalism have been elusive — hardly surprising, because it sounds as though she might have been only a part-time stringer — so we may never truly know what led to her meeting with Himmler, what happened behind closed doors, or what drove her to spy for the Nazis long after she could have walked away.

It's true that Anja never used Aldo and her concern for his future to justify her actions, but it's impossible to escape the conclusion that her desire to have him Aryanised must have played a major role. Why else would she have repeatedly risked the wrath of the world's most evil and violent men by haranguing the Nazis in Italy to speed up his paperwork? Yet there are signs that Anja's relationship with her son post-war were not good.

Anja mentioned Aldo in her reparation application, giving an address for him in Dusseldorf — but she made no further comment. Given that she referred only to visiting Freiburg, it could be inferred that the pair did not see each other much after the war. Records show that Aldo continued to reside in the city until at least 1965, when his occupation was listed as Auslandskorr — foreign correspondent. Where he worked and for whom has been impossible to establish, but it seems he did not want to live close to either his mother or father, even though he followed in his mother's professional footsteps as a journalist. It's possible that he was angry at Hans' infidelity while married to his mother. Aldo could also be forgiven for resenting his mother's collaboration with the persecutors of the Jews, even if she ostensibly did it to protect him.

Then again, such an assumption might be entirely misplaced. Aldo wrote a letter to Der Spiegel in 1953, on the subject of the Hitler Oath — taken by all soldiers — and an article by the Communist journalist Alfred Andersch, a man who had been imprisoned in Dachau, albeit for a month, and served in and then deserted the Wehrmacht. By a twist of fate, Andersch had been a pupil at the Wittelsbacher Gymnasium back in 1928, when Himmler's father was the headmaster. Andersch had even been expelled for arguing with the man.

In his piece, Andersch had argued that the Hitler Oath was "null and void," and as a result there had been nothing wrong with soldiers who surrendered or deserted. In his response, Aldo called Hitler a "demon," but pointed out that: "One does not serve a man, but the nation. It was to this nation that one took the oath." Aldo's point was not exactly clear, but he appeared to be expressing frustration with those who had 'betrayed' the oath by laying down their arms. Perhaps it suggests that he had grown up not fully aware — or not accepting the truth — of his heritage. It might also suggest that his mother had, in the end, become a genuine Nazi and passed her views onto her son.

While Anja's true leanings will probably never be known, it has since been pointed out by some of the Bergroth family's descendants that her sister Judith despised Hitler. Indeed, at one point she managed to get her family out of Hitler's Germany and back to Helsinki only to be evacuated back to the Reich amid Soviet bombing. This had involved taking a great personal risk by making a personal request to take her children out of their obligatory Hitler Youth organisations. Judith later worked for military intelligence, mainly censoring letters, but was fired in 1941 for what her son later called "political unreliability". Her husband, a leading lawyer, had previously turned down the chairmanship of Hamburg's Nazi lawyer's association amid his fury at the Nuremberg Laws. The decision had effectively ended his career, a few years before he died from pneumonia. Anja could likewise have despised the Nazis while recognizing that she had to find a way to survive within the system.

Besides the issues of loyalty both to her son and the Nazi ideology, Anja was clearly afflicted by good, old-fashioned greed. Ever since she had saved her father and her sister's fiancé from inflicting further damage upon each other, and perhaps others, during the gun fight in Helsinki, Anja had always known how to survive and prosper. She bankrupted Hans Götz with outlandish demands for alimony — probably using her illness as a justification — then fleeced Baron Manfredi for all she could get. Finally, she obtained at least 300,000 lire from the SD, whose operatives were under direct orders to pay almost anything she asked.

While Anja was able to induce her Nazi paymasters to part with ever-increasing quantities of cash, when it came to fulfilling Himmler's secret mission, Anja self-sabotaged. She was repeatedly told to be discreet and to keep a low profile while awaiting her Swiss visa in Milan. Instead, she bragged and boasted of her association with Himmler, and more than likely made friends with partisans. In fact, she kept such a high and unsavoury profile that her visa application was inevitably refused. Cynics might note that throughout this period of good living, her health did not appear to suffer and her time spent unable to leave the country coincided with time during which she did not seem to need any expensive medical treatment.

As Klaus Hügel suggested, was Anja really just a "swindler" who pulled off a remarkable fraud against the leader of the SS, stringing him along with promises that she couldn't — or wouldn't — keep while soliciting large sums of money from him?

It's highly unlikely that Anja was a Soviet spy, as Baron Manfredi's mother alleged. Nothing has yet been uncovered in Russian archives to suggest that she was, and if the Soviets had managed to place a spy so close to Himmler then they almost certainly would have publicly celebrated the achievement at some point after the war. There is no indication that Anja ever visited the Soviet Union for training, nor that she would have been capable of keeping such a mission secret.

On the other hand, there is no escaping the implication of her closeness to the Finnish establishment, in particular her 'uncle' Onni Talas. Working under diplomatic protection in Rome, if the Finns were running any sort of espionage campaign in the country, Talas would most certainly have had a hand in it. Common sense suggests that Anja would at least have passed on information if she was asked.

But was she formally working as a Felix Kersten-style agent of influence for Finland? It remains plausible that she was intentionally injected into Himmler's life by a government that already knew how easily he could be manipulated. But again, Anja was not particularly subtle and it's doubtful whether she would have been able to keep up such a charade. In any case, there is no firm evidence either way.

Alongside Anja's motivations and intentions, there is the question of her historical significance in the context of Himmler's and the Third Reich's final days. It could be said that Anja nearly played as significant a role as the likes of Baron Parilli, Felix Kersten or Count Bernadotte, insofar as that she could have been used by Himmler to extend peace feelers, or by Finland to influence Himmler, or as some other conduit between the Allies and the many Nazis of whom she was acquainted. In the event, it seems that Anja got absolutely nowhere with her espionage career, beyond undertaking a few minor missions. Her greatest successes seem to have been in engineering situations whereby she could obtain more personal funds.

We do not know if the relationship between Anja and Himmler was ever sexual, although Anja certainly tried to give Hügel the impression that it was. We do know that after her arrest in Italy she was able to demand an audience with Himmler and, apparently, get one. Therefore, Anja's potential influence over the SS-Reichsführer at a critical stage of the conflict shouldn't be undersold.

Himmler was one of the most powerful men in the Nazi hierarchy, arguably the most powerful given his absolute personal control over the SS, but he was also highly susceptible to manipulation. Taken in the context of what is known about Himmler's efforts to open negotiations with the Allies, it's surely no coincidence that Himmler wanted to send Anja on a "special mission" to Switzerland at exactly the same time that he was trying to open discussions with the Allies there. Anja would have been the perfect tool — a non-Nazi but an admirer of Himmler who could also speak of having a Jewish husband and son, she was eminently well-connected within diplomatic and artistic circles, as well as with Jewish refugees such as Seligman and Plesch. Anja would have been able to open channels with any number of Western figures in the country. She might even have been carrying a written offer hidden in the code of her unplayable sheet music. Himmler must have had a very specific task in mind — one for which he was prepared to expend political capital by admonishing subordinates who doubted Anja's value.

While Anja had never been a candidate for Wolf and Zimmer's Operation Wool, Himmler clearly intended to use her for his own schemes. We now know that she served at least one other purpose — Himmler thought she held sprawling estates somewhere in Finland where he might be able to hide out after the war. Did this reliable-sounding back-up plan, which he discussed with his astrologer when the proverbial hit the fan, embolden Himmler in his treacherous dealings with the Jewish groups and the Allies? If it did, Anja would have been oblivious to this side-effect of her confidence trick.

There is one last unanswered question, concerning Anja's contacts with the Italian resistance and exactly what role she might have played there. It's possible that she became a double agent for the rebels as Zimmer's interest in his spy network wavered. Given that Anja spent months openly boasting of her friendship with Himmler, we must assume that she held some value for the partisans, otherwise she would surely have faced detention, or worse, at the end of the war. Instead, according to Manfredi family lore, when the conflict ended she openly remained on the Italian Riviera, close to Aldo, still living the high life. Until, that is, Giacomo arrived to confront her — Anja had stashed the family jewels in a hotel safe and was living off the credit. Filippo's younger brother ruthlessly took them back.

If only Klaus Hügel had succeeded in getting his hands on that suspicious musical manuscript, perhaps we would have more answers to the many mysteries surrounding Anja Bergroth Manfredi de Blasiis. She has few living relatives, none of whom have been able to shed much light on her life. Her son Aldo died in January 1997. Anja's niece Anja Stromfeldt married in Ohio, USA, in May 1947, to an ex-US serviceman. She died in Texas in 1993. Anja's sister Judith also died, in Stockholm, in September that year. A relative studying family genealogy found out that a cousin, Richard Winter, had met Anja in Stockholm on a few occasions after the war. Judith and her son Kurt were also there regularly. But he could remember little else of note for this story.

Anja deserves her place in the history books, and not merely as Himmler's 'other' mistress. While we may never know the true extent of her contribution towards the SD's efforts in Italy, they were probably not significant. It is therefore fair to say that Anja Manfredi should be remembered less as a Nazi spy, and more as a particularly gifted fraudster, a swindler in the words of Klaus Hügel. But we know that Anja must have exerted a great deal of influence upon Himmler. Clearly, she did not use her position of influence to free prisoners. But she was on Himmler's mind right up until the fall of the Nazi regime. We can only guess at how Himmler's unwavering faith in this most unreliable of secret agents might have affected his thinking in those final days, as he cynically sought to save Jewish lives and end the war in his favour. Perhaps, in a typically strange and roundabout way, Anja did help to do some good.

And while Anja was, without doubt, a crook, she also had a second motivation, which should not be underestimated — the protection of her son. Even the monstrous Heinrich Himmler seemed to understand as much when he addressed her by the apparently affectionate nickname — The German mother.

---

[56] Margerete Himmler files.
[57] Himmler files.
[58] Hügel files.
[59] See Jaeger.
[60] Anja Manfredi files, German archives.

Bibliography

Archive files

BEETZ, HILDEGARD, Volume 1. Record Group 263: Records of the Central Intelligence Agency, 1894 - 2002.
Link: https://catalog.archives.gov/id/139315871

BEETZ, HILDEGARD, Volume 2. Record Group 263: Records of the Central Intelligence Agency, 1894 - 2002.
Link: https://catalog.archives.gov/id/139316221

Blasiis, Manfredi Anja , Baroness (née Bergroth), born in Helsingfor (Finland). 1959-1964, State Archives Baden-Württemberg.

Filippo MANFREDI DE BLASIS: Italian. Baron Filippo MANFREDI DE BLASIS was suspected of being a German spy intended to operate behind Allied lines when the Germans retreated to Northern Italy. KV 2/1940. National Archives, Kew.

HUEGEL, KLAUS. Record Group 263: Records of the Central Intelligence Agency, 1894 - 2002.
Link: https://catalog.archives.gov/id/139351414

Mrs Margherita HIMMLER and daughter (wife and daughter of Reichsführer-SS Heinrich HIMMLER): capture and disposal. WO 204/12603. National Archives, Kew.

PARILLI, LUIGI. Record Group 263: Records of the Central Intelligence Agency, 1894 - 2002.
Link: https://catalog.archives.gov/id/139382609

RAUFF, WALTER. Record Group 263: Records of the Central Intelligence Agency, 1894 - 2002.
Link: https://catalog.archives.gov/id/139386909

SS Sturmbannführer Dr Klaus HÜGEL. WO 204/12795. National Archives, Kew.

Walter Friedrich SCHELLENBERG: rose to be No. 2 in the S.D. and was close to Himmler. Files KV 2/94, KV 2/95, KV 2/96, KV 2/97, KV 2/98, KV 2/99. National Archives, Kew.

ZIMMER, GUIDO. Record Group 263: Records of the Central Intelligence Agency, 1894 - 2002.
Link: https://catalog.archives.gov/id/16971904

Books

Bernadotte, Folke. (2009). Last Days of the Reich, the Diary of Count Folke Bernadotte. Frontline Books.

Bonsdorff, Axel von. (1941). Släkten Bonsdorff - von Bonsdorff jämte ättlingar. Helsingfors. Släkten Bonsdorff.

Dulles, Allen. (2006). The Secret Surrender. The Lyons Press.

Hoare, Oliver. (2000). Camp 020, MI5 and the Nazi Spier. Public Record Office.

Katz, Robert. (1967). Death in Rome. Jonathan Cape.

Kessel, Joseph. (1961). The Magic Touch. Hart-Davis.

Lamb, Richard. (1996). War in Italy 1943-1945, A Brutal Story. Da Capo Press.

Longerich, Peter. (2012) Heinrich Himmler. Oxford University Press.

Manes, Philipp. (2009). As If It Were Life. A WWII Diary From The Theresienstadt Ghetto. Palgrave Macmillan.

Plesch, Janos. (1948). Janos: The Story of a Doctor. Victor Gollancz.

Sands, Philippe. (2020). The Ratline, Love Lies and Justice on the Trail of a Nazi Fugitive. Weidenfeld and Nicholson.

Schellenberg, Walter. (2000). The Labyrinth: Memoirs of Walter Schellenberg, Hitler's Chief of Counterintelligence. Da Capo Press.

Wallace, Max. (2018) In the Name of Humanity, The Secret Deal to End the Holocaust. (Skyhorse Publishing).

Waller, John. (2002). The Devil's Doctor, Felix Kersten and the Secret Plot to Turn Himmler Against Hitler. John Wiley & Sons.

Wulff, Wilhelm. (1973). Zodiac and the Swastika. Coward, McCann & Geoghegan. New York.

Wyllie, James. (2019. Nazi Wives, the Women at the Top of Hitler's Germany. The History Press.

Online articles

Blodsramat I Helsingfors. Åbo Underrättelser, September 29, 1915. Link: https://digi.kansalliskirjasto.fi/sanomalehti/binding/1162110?term=Bergroth&term=Gunnar%20Aspelin&term=Bergroths&page=4

Götz, Aldo. Letter to Der Spiegel, January 7, 1953.
Link: https://magazin.spiegel.de/EpubDelivery/spiegel/pdf/25655541

Hurt, Raymond. (2004). Tuberculosis sanatorium regimen in the 1940s: a patient's personal diary. Journal of the Royal Society of Medicine.
Link: https://www.ncbi.nlm.nih.gov/pmc/articles/PMC1079536/

Jaeger, Roland (2011). Torre zur Bucherwelt: Hamburgs Antiquariate und Auktionshauser der Zwischenkriegszeit (II). Aus dem Antiquariat NF 9, Nr 1.

Survivors Remember Kristallnacht: Johanna (Gerechter) Neumann : https://www.youtube.com/watch?v=Z69qY5s7Yas

Theresienstadt Ghetto.
Link: https://www.theholocaustexplained.org/the-camps/theresienstadt-a-case-study/cultural-life-within-theresienstadt/

Theresienstadt. United States Holocaust Memorial Museum.
Link: https://encyclopedia.ushmm.org/content/en/article/theresienstadt

Theresienstadt. Yad Vasehm.

Link:
https://www.yadvashem.org/holocaust/about/ghettos/theresienstadt.ht
ml

Ulrike Sparr (2005). ELSBET FLORA GÖTZ, Stolperstein Hamburg.
Link:
https://www.stolpersteine-
hamburg.de/index.php?MAIN_ID=7&BIO_ID=954)

Index

ABOUT THE AUTHOR

 John Lucas has written for some of Britain's best-selling national newspapers, including *The Sun*, *The Daily Mirror*, the *Mail on Sunday* and *The Times*. He is also the author of three more books:

Britain's Forgotten Serial Killer — Tells the chilling life story of one of Britain's most notorious murderers, Patrick Mackay, and a string of unsolved crimes for which he remains the prime suspect.

Albanian Mafia Wars: The Rise of Europe's Deadliest Narcos — Exposes the untold saga of one of the world's newest and most dangerous criminal societies, from the civil strife of the Balkans to the streets of New York and the tower blocks of East London.

Dope Kings of London: Brilliant Chang, Eddie Manning, and Secrets of the First War on Drugs — The tale of a loose network of original narcos who shipped cocaine, heroin, and other drugs around the world in the wake of the first anti-narcotics laws.

Also published by Aberfeldy London:

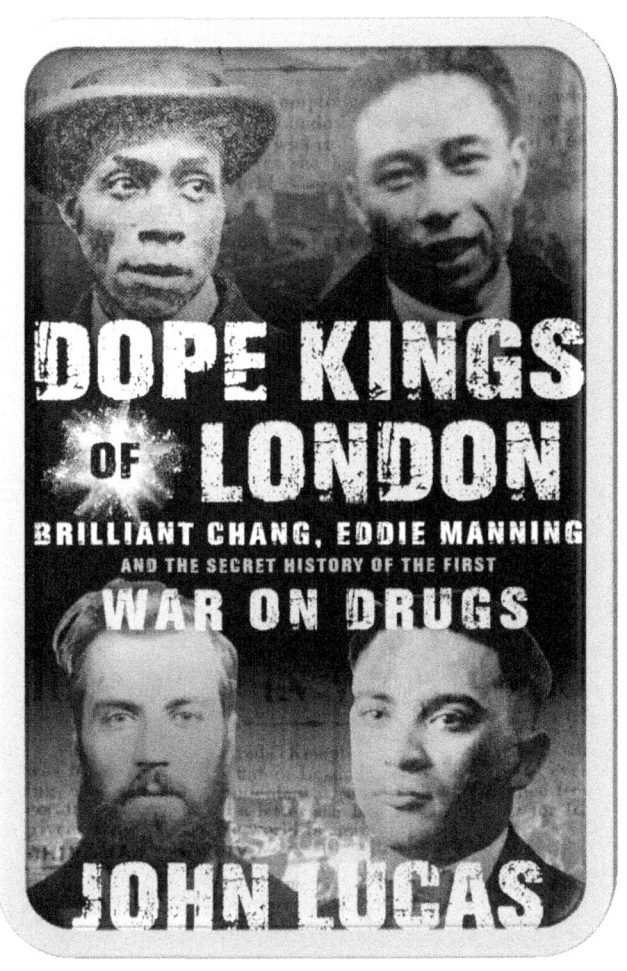

Printed in Great Britain
by Amazon

40716761R00121